What readers are saying about
In This Small Place...

"My sense of the history of the area where I have lived my life was greatly magnified when I read this book. I loved it. I can't believe we now have a historical resource like this. Actually, it is extraordinary."

—Steve Thompson,
Retired history teacher,
writer and Civil War expert

"*In This Small Place* is local history at its best. Eddie Ellis is to be commended for his path-breaking research, his historical skills and his storytelling."

—Dr. David S. Cecelski
Author and professor of history
UNC-CH and Duke University

"From peaches floating in moonshine to center-of-town hog lots to the then-pristine shores of our creeks and rivers, Ellis paints a picture of life here over the past 300 years. His easy, conversational style reminds the reader of his years of experience speaking to historical and school groups about the subject close to his heart—his hometown of Havelock...Readers will be truly amazed."

—Hunter Bretzius
Associate Publisher/Executive Editor
Havelock News

"There were many times...when I had to put the book down and wipe my eyes as I laughed out loud at the colorful way he weaves his magic."

—Skip Crayton
Author of *Remember When*

In This Small Place

Amazing Tales of the First 300 Years of Havelock and Craven County, North Carolina

EDWARD BARNES ELLIS, JR.

McBryde Publishing
New Bern, North Carolina USA

In This Small Place

Published by McBryde Publishing, Inc.
New Bern, North Carolina

Set in Bookman Old Style
Manufactured in the United States of America

Library of Congress Cataloguing-in-Publication Data
Ellis, Edward Barnes, Jr., In this small place
ISBN 0-9758700-1-7

Second Printing: October, 2005

Cover Concept by the Author
Cover Design: Danielle Bouffard and Bill Benners
Front Cover Art: Antique Print
"Gathering Turpentine in the Forests of North Carolina"

For a dedicated historian and genealogist,
my uncle,
Charles Brantley Ellis, Sr.

Contents

NOTE ON SPELLING

Spellings appear inconsistent throughout this book simply because they have changed through the years.

For example, Slocum used to be Slocumbe and was later spelled Slocumb. We have found it spelled Slokum and Slocom as well. Slocum Creek used to be Slocum's Creek and Slocumb's Creek. Hancock was spelled Handcock in colonial times. The modern Wynne was spelled Wynn and Winn. Always is frequently spelled Allways, sometimes (but not always) both ways in the same document. We found local land holder William Wicheliff's last name spelled in three variations in the same deed, circa 1790.

Mostly, when talking about the old days, the old spelling is used. In talking about the present, we usually use the current spelling. But, on occasion, we have switched back and forth between the two arbitrarily and without warning or embarrassment.

Acknowledgements

First of all, I urge the reader's support of the Havelock Historical Preservation Society. Their work is vital. Their accomplishments will be a gift to all future generations.

With regards to this book I send sincere thanks to John B. Green, III who introduced me to the Bryan Prospectus many years ago. John is a tireless researcher, author, historian, and reference librarian at the Kellenberger Room of the New Bern-Craven County Library. He read the book, answered many questions and helped make it better.

Thanks also to local native David S. Cecelski, distinguished professor of history at Duke University and UNC-Chapel Hill, for offering his valuable support.

My old friend Warren Nye, a genuinely skilled journalist, carefully edited the first draft of the manuscript. Any errors remaining are mine, not his, as I kept making changes after he had done his excellent job.

For their support, friendship, contributions and efforts, I also wish to thank retired Havelock High School history teacher and Civil War expert Steve Thompson; attorney Bobby Stricklin, the legal wizard who taught me how to get the most from county records; Hunter Bretzius, ENC Publications, for her input on the manuscript; Barbara Thompson for loving history wherever she finds it; my daughter, Beth Ellis DeMarco, for her excellent ideas and suggestions; Bill Benners for many long hours of editorial and technical magic; and Skip

Crayton for lighting the path to authorship and publication.

Though they are no longer with us, my warm regards for contributions and inspiration extend to Charlie Markey, Markey Advertising and Printing, a Havelock booster and pioneer businessman who shared his local historical knowledge and treasures with me; Dick Tuttle, who truly loved this place and worked to make it better; Arthur W. Edwards, school administrator, principal, educator, motivator and devotee of history; and the one and only Irving Beck, another essential business pioneer, town founder and a role model for role models.

Special thanks to the William L. Clements Library, University of Michigan, for permission to use portions of the previously unpublished *Levi Kent Journal*.

Finally, I offer my deepest appreciation to my wife, Veronica. Not only does she indulge my history habit and odd work schedule, but also spent long hours providing useful and detailed feedback on the book's readability. Thank you, Ronnie.

Foreword

When most of us think of history books, we reflect back to courses in college or high school — books crammed with dates and statistics. Most authors in this genre, if it can be called that, spend more time dealing with facts than breathing life into the stories. There are exceptions with writers like David McCullough who writes history for the enjoyment of reading. Like McCullough, Eddie Ellis has been able to bridge the gap of textbook writing and bring the history of Havelock, North Carolina and Craven County to the forefront, by painting a visual picture, much like what is found in modern novels. In the first chapter, his writing captures the comparison to skiffs and bicycles better than the picture that introduces that chapter.

The reason that Ellis is so adept at showing the fascinating history of his "Small Place," is the fact that he is no stranger to the written word. For years, he was publisher and editor of the Havelock News. It was during that tenure that Ellis became the historian of his hometown. His research is as professional as his writing, as the hundreds of documents he processes will testify.

As someone who has called Craven County home for most of my life, I have only appreciated Havelock as home to the economic engine that drives the eastern part of the state; that along with loathing the gauntlet of stoplights that make a trip to the beach a stressful drive. It is through the writing of Eddie Ellis that I have come to appreciate the importance his part of our state shared with the rest of the nation—from Burnside amphibious landing during the battle of New Bern to the business of shipbuilding, whose demise gave way to a bootlegging industry that flourished long before the good ole boys from Boone and Asheville ever learned the trade.

To say that *In This Small Place* reads like a novel would sell short the accurate blending of history and storytelling Eddie Ellis brings to this wonderful book. But there were many times, however, when I had to put the book down and wipe my eyes as I laughed out loud at the colorful way he weaved his magic. At other times I felt the bone-chilling cold as a Yankee soldier shivered face down in freezing water to avoid the musket balls being hailed in his direction.

For years the history of New Bern has dominated Craven County and overshadowed the other communities. With this book, Eddie Ellis has painted a portrait revealing how Havelock has made a much larger contribution to that history than ever previously thought and how this "Small Place" continues to do so today.

— Skip Crayton, author of *Remember When*

We live in the past by knowledge of its history, and in the future by hope and anticipation. By ascending to an association with our ancestors; by contemplating their example and studying their character; by partaking their sentiments and imbibing their spirit; by accompanying them in their toils; by sympathizing in their suffering and rejoicing in their successes and triumphs, we mingle our existence with theirs and seem to belong to their age.

— Daniel Webster

A people which take no pride in the noble achievements of remote ancestors will never achieve anything worthy to be remembered by remote ancestors.

— Lord Macauley

In This
Small Place

In the good old Meuse.

1
A Story to Tell

In the small, grainy, black and white photograph, a young girl stands barefoot in the stern of a boat. The boat is a short handmade rowing skiff, the kind that used to be as common here as a bicycle. It is a sunny day. She is wearing a simple skirt and blouse. A straw hat covers her head. Near her in the calm, shallow water is another girl, possibly a sister. The second girl stands calf deep in the river holding a homemade crab net with a short wooden handle. She is wearing an old-fashioned sailor blouse, a skirt and a broad-brimmed straw hat. She is smiling.

The girls' images reflect on the surface of the water. The river's soft tranquillity surrounds them and the boat. It stretches to the grainy horizon as still as a mirror, as smooth as glass.

At the bottom of the old photograph, along the white border of the print, someone has penned a few words in a lovely script. It reads "in the good old Neuse."

For the individuals who peopled this place for so long, the Neuse River and its surrounding forests always gave generously. The basic necessities of survival could be had here. For the early settlers, these natural blessings of the river and the woods were the source of life-giving sustenance and, more rarely, wealth. It was the big river and the deep woods, after all, that drew them here from the very beginning.

The good old Neuse, indeed.

Today, it is difficult to fathom that Havelock is a waterfront community. This is simply because the Cherry Point Marine Corps Air Station now occupies the riverfront. Nevertheless, for most of its existence, people at this place have lived with, lived by, and lived from the river and its connecting creeks. The Neuse River and the creeks, principally Slocum, Hancock, Tucker, Anderson, and Clubfoot, have provided transportation, food, and recreation for generation upon generation.

If you look closely you will see that modern Havelock is cut in two places by water. One is at the "three bridges" on U.S. 70 near the current U.S. Post Office. The other is at Dick Parker Ford near the main gate of the base. If you follow either downstream for a short distance these two prongs of Slocum Creek become navigable and join together at the point near Graham A. Barden Elementary School. How navigable? In 1862, the Union navy drove a steamship full of soldiers from the Neuse River all the way to where the elementary school is today. You could have easily heard the ship's whistle from Main Street.

A little farther downstream Slocum Creek widens and is joined by creeks called Tucker and Anderson and soon the whole shebang flows spectacularly between two lovely sand beaches into one of the broadest rivers in the country. The Neuse River is nearly three miles wide at Havelock.

If you stood today at the crossroads intersection in the middle of town and could be magically lifted a mere 100 feet in the air, looking north, you would see it all. Water, water, everywhere.

Slocum Creek is on the western side of the Marine base. On its east side, Hancock Creek performs the same routine. It flows from a tiny stream that runs under Highway 101 at the first big curve on the way to Beaufort. Very quickly downstream it squares its shoulders and, joined by other creeks, broadens into a navigable tributary of the Neuse. Cherry Point is surrounded on three sides by water.

Slocum, Hancock, and Clubfoot, three of the parallel "creeks" on the southern edge of the river, are so large they would be called rivers anywhere else in the country. We call them creeks simply because the Neuse River is so enormous.

Not so long ago, every resident here had an intimate knowledge of all this water. As much as the dirt roads through the forest, the creeks and river functioned as highways. They were the source of a variety of fish, crabs, and clams. They were the playground as well. People lived and worked by and on the water. To get around, to fish, and to transport goods, everyone had a flat-bottom skiff, a canoe, or a sailboat.

Today we have mostly forgotten all this. For better or for worse, we have severed our connection with a way of life that went on here for hundreds of years. We will attempt in this book to reconnect with these by-gone days. A key to this is visualizing the time when people paddled their boats, pulled their nets, and watched the evening colors change on the water of the good old Neuse.

So, who were these people?

There was a time, in the not-too-distant past, when the names of local families included Thorpe, Tucker, Glover, Slocumb, Lovick, Whitehead, Fisher, Potter, Benners, Neale, Loftin, Handcock, Holton, Masters, Physioc, Pearson, Routledge, Jones, Evans,

Winn, Corbins, Always, Ellis, Green, Barnes and Bishop. Today, except for some Fisher and Winn (Wynne) descendents, almost no one from these families is here.

The story of where they went and where all the rest of us came from is the history of the place we call Havelock.

At its essence, history, after all, is about people; not about places or things. It is about men and women and children, who lived and breathed, loved and married, acquired and built, fought and died. All of that has gone on here. And much, much more.

In fact, the story of this little backwoods crossroads is absolutely incredible. It has fascinated me since childhood and has been my hobby, my avocation, and, at times, my passion. I have been thrilled by what I have "discovered" and sometimes I have been saddened by it.

Now this is not to say that our town is unusual in this respect. The fact is that you can go anywhere—anywhere—and scratch the surface and discover the same kind of stories. People are amazing. They can and will do anything. The thing to know is that they have done it, all of it, right here where we are now—in Havelock, North Carolina.

There is a tendency when viewing history to think of the people in it as somehow unreal, as characters in a work of fiction. It is important to grasp, to really think about and absorb the fact, that all of the people who came to the Neuse River basin since 1690 felt the sun and rain upon their skin, were scratched by greenbriers as they walked through the woods, experienced fear at noises in the night, and gloried at the vision of the moon rising over the water, just as we do today. Remember this.

It is also important to remember that there were already people here. A thriving population of the Tuscarora clan, including the local Neusioks and Corees, descendants of Asian wanderers who walked and sailed to what we now call North America over the course of perhaps 35,000 years. They had forgotten that they came from other places. They thought that they had always been here and had stories based on the belief that the place had been created just for them. Their villages and settlements dotted the region. They were interconnected by trade and marriage and squabbles just like the rest of us.

But like the Thorpes, the Slocumbs, and the others, they are gone, too.

So, where did they go?

If you wonder that, if you wonder just that much, then you may have what it takes to sit still long enough for me to tell you some of what I have learned over the course of the past 45 years about this small place that we call Havelock, that the settlers called Slocumb's Creek, and that the Indians called God knows what.

Here is my caveat: I am not a professional historian. What formal training I have is mostly in business and journalism. You will find no footnotes here, and only a few references to source documents. I am simply a curious amateur.

Without my advance knowledge, on February 27, 1984, the city board, on a motion by Commissioner Lee K. Allen, seconded by Commissioner Richard Rice, voted unanimously to make me the official historian for the City of Havelock. The honor came with a decree signed by City Clerk Vira Watson and a black metal filing cabinet, which I still have. I was informed of the appointment when I was contacted by a reporter from an out-of-town newspaper who wanted my reaction. No one ever told me what precipitated the vote, but I assumed that some word had leaked out somewhere of my otherwise private obsession with local past events. In any event, it was a great kindness and I appreciate it to this day. But even this official sanction adds no horsepower to my credentials as a historian.

Details of what I say here may be proven wrong at some future moment. The tale I offer will be out of order; sometimes slightly incoherent. Some of this is surmise, theory, and conjecture. And there are gaps. The story is surely incomplete. History always is.

There are some things we do not know. There are some things we cannot know. There is mystery, and life is richer for it. To future historians for whom I muddy the water, I herewith offer my apologies. But I promise that the things I am going to tell you are true to the best of my meager knowledge and skills.

You may wonder where all the information in this book came from. It has come, over many years, from national, state, and university archives. It has come, one fact at a time, from libraries, from courthouses, and from interviews with individuals. In some cases, it has been found on foot. Most recently, the Internet has been a great blessing. Unless I tell you in the text that I am guessing, all of the numbers, facts, and claims contained herein are backed up by material in my collection of documents, books, and photographs.

In the telling of this story we visit other places of course. We have long been tied by water, dirt road, rail, and now highway to New Bern, Harlowe, Newport, Morehead City and Beaufort. We must look to each of them for some of what we are. We will look many places. We seek knowledge and understanding.

So, here we go.

One of the first things to understand is that in the 1800s a huge shift in international technology threw a monkey wrench into the gears of the local economy. This calamity caused most of the early settlers to leave Havelock and was the catalyst for the creation of our famous illegal liquor industry. To see how this happened the first place we must look is the Civil War.

2

Why the Yankees Invaded Havelock

$\mathscr{T}$he Civil War, hmmm?

Being, as they say, by the grace of God a Southern boy, I actually much prefer The War Between the States or even The War of Northern Aggression. My grandmother lived on the Neuse River between New Bern and Havelock. When she was a child she had living relatives with personal memories of the war. When I was a child she used to point at my belly button and tell me that was "where the Yankees shot you," which delighted me to no end. As children, my father and his brothers played under their Goldsboro home with boxes of Confederate money, saved, I guess, in case the South should rise again. But all that is politics and since this is a book of history I will steer clear of it.

Suffice it to say that in 1861, President Abraham Lincoln had himself a terrible problem. Saddled with the most bone-headed collection of generals ever, Lincoln could not buy a victory. Since the fall of Fort Sumter, South Carolina, in April of that year, every time his Union forces tried to come south, the pesky rebels handed the President's men their hats back with their heads still in them.

Lincoln needed a battlefield victory. He was an unpopular President in an unpopular war. He needed some good news. He needed a win. He needed a foothold in the south and he needed it quickly. Ambrose Burnside was about to give him all of that.

Burnside was a little peacock of a man. He loved to strut around the dirt streets of Washington, D.C., grinning broadly in his stylish uniform with all his medals gleaming and, despite his tiny frame, considered himself quite the ladies' man. He also had what I have described to school children as a "weird beard." He had big fluffy muttonchops that did not join at the chin. Some others emulated the style and it became known around town as "burnsides." In the wild and wonderful ways of the American language this has been twisted around over the years. So now you can win bar bets with the knowledge that Major General Ambrose Burnside, the soon-to-be invader of Havelock, is credited as the namesake of sideburns.

But I digress.

Lincoln asked Gen. Burnside for a plan and Burnside suggested the thing to do would be to assemble a fleet of ships and sail to one of the least populated and most desolate regions of the Confederate seaboard. There they would encounter little resistance, would be behind the lines of General Robert E. Lee's rebel forces in Virginia and would open a port where Union forces could come and go as they pleased. This would form a base of Southern operations, would demoralize, or at least worry and aggravate, the enemy and would give Lincoln the victory he so sorely needed.

Lacking other options, Lincoln put his support behind the Burnside invasion.

Here things bogged down. It took Burnside nearly a year to assemble his dozens of ships, his thousands of troopers, and his tons upon tons of weapons and supplies.

Eng. by H.B. Hall's Sons New York

Gen. Ambrose E. Burnside

Edward Ellis Collection

While Burnside is working on getting his invasion together, let's spend a few moments pondering why eastern North Carolina was so unpopulated and desolate.

We will go back further in time. Imagine you are a shoemaker who wants a new life in America. You have boarded a small, leaky wooden sailing ship in London in, say, 1753 and are about to voyage across the ocean—across the ocean!—with your precious family and all your worldly goods. Perhaps the captain gives you your choice of sailing to:

1) The Port of Boston, or
2) The Port of Charleston, or
3) "The Graveyard of the Atlantic."

Which would you choose?

Trust me; Number Three was an unpopular selection.

The long, curving coast of North Carolina, the aforementioned "Graveyard," has always had a string of barrier islands broken only by a series of shifting and treacherous inlets. Add to that three sets of shoals running straight out into the sea; Diamond Shoals off Cape Hatteras, Cape Lookout Shoals off Beaufort, and Frying Pan Shoals off Wilmington. In some places, the water may only be six inches deep many miles offshore. They did not call it "Cape Fear" for nothing. Add to that the frequency of hurricanes and the powerful Gulf Stream, a river of warm water in the ocean driving northward with its foggy, stormy weather, and you wind up with more shipwrecks than National Geographic can fit in tiny print on a three-foot map of the North Carolina shoreline. Pirates, like Blackbeard, called it home because few would chase them here. But even Blackbeard lost his flagship near Beaufort. Call it a destination of last resort.

Other modes of transportation, of course, were foot, horse or wagon. If you were coming from the north or south on muddy dirt roads, when you reach North Carolina you must swing wide to the west to avoid a parallel series of huge rivers with accompanying swampy terrain for miles on each side. Crossing these rivers was difficult, dangerous, and, if you had to hire someone to ferry you across, expensive. The Cape Fear, the Neuse, the Pamlico, and the Albemarle Sound were huge impediments to travel and still are. The State of North Carolina recently spent $100 million for a bridge to cross the Neuse at New Bern. Even today, to cross the river from Havelock to Pamlico County you have to go by state ferry.

So, most travelers walked far west around the rivers and few ships risked sailing here. Most settlers simply did not come here at all. President George Washington traversed the region in 1791 and wrote in his diary that in eastern North Carolina he had "passed through the most barren country I have ever beheld." Although it is rapidly changing, to this day eastern North Carolina is among the least densely populated areas from Boston to Key West.

That is why Burnside picked the Neuse River for his amphibious attack.

When the little general finally got his fleet together, the Yankees had their own problems with the Graveyard of the Atlantic. Coming around Cape Hatteras, the ships encountered a strong storm that damaged some, wrecked several, and scattered the rest. The rough seas necessitated repairs once the fleet entered the Pamlico Sound.

Getting there was not easy.

Burnside had received what turned out to be "faulty intelligence" regarding water depth at Hatteras Inlet and the fleet had great difficulty crossing the bar there. Marine First Lt. Richard A. Ward, writing a paper, in modern times, for the

Amphibious Warfare School, described the Union force's "novel method...devised to dredge a channel for the larger ships." According to Ward, the big transports "were driven onto the bar at full steam while the tide was ebbing and the anchor was carried forward by a small boat to hold the ship in position. The strong current then washed the sand from beneath the vessel, thus allowing her to make another run at the bar."

This grueling process continued for several days. At last, a channel some eight feet deep was formed allowing the bruised fleet to limp into the relative safety of Pamlico Sound. Some ships cleared the bar with only inches to spare beneath their keels. After making repairs, Burnside's force fought its first engagement, quickly taking possession of Roanoke Island. The fleet would wait now until the time was right to move on New Bern.

3
Union Fleet Foretells Change

*H*ad you been standing where the 15th green of the Carolina Pines golf course now overlooks the Neuse River early on the morning of March 13, 1862, the hair on the back of your neck would have been standing at attention. A fleet of some 60 Yankee war ships, large and small, would be arrayed before your disbelieving eyes like ghosts that had appeared during the long, cold night.

The fleet was mostly at anchor on the flat-calm water and in much activity. It focused primarily on the beaches on either side of the mouth of Slocum's Creek spanning the shore from where Carolina Pines Golf & Country Club and the Cherry Point Officers Club are today.

The Union armada covered much of the river. It has been described as a "motley one." Fourteen large transport ships were accompanied by shallow draft steamers, barges, sailboats, tugs, and ferries. During that day and some of the next, after brief cannon bombardment of the vacant shoreline, the fleet disgorged 15,000 men; more men than Gen. Douglas MacArthur would use to invade Inchon during the Korean War of the 1950s.

Burnside's spies had told him that to unload farther up the river risked damage from a carefully constructed series of Confederate forts. Past Slocum's Creek toward New Bern the river gradually narrows to the width where the fleet would have been within reach of rebel cannon fire and small arms. By off-loading where the river is two-and-a-half miles wide, below the line the rebels chose to defend, Burnside and his troops could avoid the forts facing the river and then simply march in behind them.

The first of these Confederate forts, the Croatan Works, spanned the distance from the railroad line all the way to the river where it was punctuated by Fort Dixie. Ten miles below New Bern toward Havelock, this line of earthworks was three-quarters of a mile long and would accommodate a force of 2,000 rebel defenders. Next in line was the earthen Fort Thompson where most of the fighting occurred. Of Fort Thompson's 13 cannons, 10 faced the river. Next was the unfinished Fort Allen, then Fort Ellis, and finally Fort Lane, located near Green Springs.

Most of the Union's men and materiel came ashore on the western side of the creek, landing at a substantial farm called Magnolia Plantation, in an odd, ramshackle manner. The troops were loaded into launches that looked much like lifeboats. These were lashed together in a train. The train of tied-together boats was then attached to a small shallow-draft steam vessel that would charge the shore line at full speed. The steamer would then turn away from the river beach at the last moment and simultaneously release the line to the boats. Under their own inertia, the boats would proceed to shallow water where the men would splash ashore with their gear and supplies. In a steady rain, the operation continued most of the day.

One of the curiosities of history is that Burnside brought some of his men ashore in an

Burnside's Fleet at Slocum Creek, March 13, 1862

Harper's Weekly

amphibious assault upon a beach that would one day serve as a home of the outfit that made amphibious assaults famous, the United States Marine Corps. Lt. Ward, the USMC writer mentioned above, said the movement was "essentially the same technique for which the Marine Corps is famous today." He noted that Burnside's tactic included a preparatory naval bombardment, the ship-to-shore movement of troops, the bringing ashore of artillery, the close support of the landing force by naval gunfire, and normal land warfare once ashore.

For the record, this was the second amphibious landing of the war. The first, also by Burnside, was at Roanoke Island the previous month.

An 1878 chart shows a huge structure immediately east of Slocum's Creek labeled "Burnside's Wharf." Local tradition has it that the big dock was carried away in a hurricane in the late 1800s. The bulk of the force landed, we now know, west of the creek.

An artist for *Harper's Weekly* was there as Burnside's troops came ashore. *Harper's Weekly* was the *USA Today* of the civil war era. In those days, artists' engraved renderings served the same purpose photographs currently do. *Harper's* had already written many articles and published many engravings of and about the preparation of Burnside's fleet.

The invasion plan was hardly a secret. In fact, *Harper's Weekly* had published several drawings of the fleet while it was assembling and named the ships that would sail south. Over the following months, the national weekly published engravings of scenes from the Burnside Expedition that led to the fall of the ports of New Bern and Beaufort, as well as the recapture of Fort Macon. There were

Union troops landing at Slocum Creek, March 13, 1862

Harper's Weekly

scenes from the fierce and bloody Battle of New Bern that resulted in nearly 1,100 casualties on March 14. Also shown were illustrations of massive Confederate earthwork forts along the Neuse. Several engravings show the landing at Slocum's Creek and the fleet assembled there.

And here is the important part: In those *Harper's Weekly* engravings of 1862 half of the fleet consists of wooden ships powered by sail; the other half, including ships colossal and petite, are powered by steam and made mostly of iron.

This is the technological shift noted at the end of Chapter One.

This change from the ancient and venerable power of the winds to the new, noisy steam engine power is the monkey that threw the wrench that killed the economy of Havelock.

Despite appearances, we are not recounting the War Between the States here. What we are driving at is that the Burnside fleet reflected "the state of the art" in marine transportation for its day. And the State of the Art was changing rapidly. The future was not ships of wood, but ships of iron and ships of steel. Wooden ships with sails were yesterday's technology. What was coming was iron construction, screw propulsion and steam power.

The invasion was bad enough for Havelock. The composition of the invasion fleet was worse, because it boldly illustrated, as we shall see, that the industry the local citizenry had depended on for more than a century was in deep, deep trouble. Like the business of the guy who was the biggest manufacturer of buggy whips when the automobile was invented, Havelock's reason for being was about to disappear.

4

Good Times, Bad Times

*R*emember history class in school, a painful memory for most no doubt, when the teacher tried to tell you about "naval stores?" Remember tar, pitch and turpentine? Does that ring a bell? Well, it should because it was one of the great industries of early America.

These products were used in the building and maintenance of wooden sailing ships. And there was big money in it.

The Havelock district was settled before the founding of New Bern in 1710. By the time of the Civil War, the people here had depended on a woodlands-based economy for 150 years. The little community spread from the mouths of Slocum Creek and Hancock Creek to where the railroad tracks crossed the Beaufort Road, today called Miller Blvd. It consisted of scores of families squeezing a living from the earth and the local pine forests. More than a few families lived quite comfortably with incomes based on naval stores and timber production.

At the time, no sailing ship left port without its essential naval stores of tar, pitch and timber.

Tar, pitch, turpentine, spirits of turpentine and rosin are made from the sap-like gum of pine trees. The Long Leaf Pine was preferred and particularly productive. To collect the gum, the outer layers of pine trees were slashed. The gum oozed from the wounds into cavities called "boxes" that were cut into the trees. The thick, gooey semi-liquid was periodically dipped into barrels and distilled and redistilled to make the various products used to seal and coat seams of wooden ships. The indispensable products prevented and controlled leaks, preserved the wood, and coated shipboard rope lines to keep them from rotting.

So ubiquitous were the products that sailors themselves would be continually stained with them. Sailors in the British navy were known as "tars." And, of course, here in the "Land of the Long Leaf Pine" beginning in colonial times, North Carolinians were nicknamed "tar heels."

Ships' masts and spars are also included in the category of naval stores. Timber for these was also produced locally.

While the soil in eastern Craven County has never been as good for agriculture as neighboring counties, the wet acid soils here grow one heck of a pine tree. In 1856, William Benjamin Thorpe's widow, Elizabeth, living on what is now Cherry Point, described their land in an estate filing this way: "The Lands aforesaid are not adapted to agricultural purposes except a small portion;...it is adapted almost exclusively to tar and turpentine..."

In the mid-1800s, 90 percent of the world's supply of naval stores came from the United States. Nearly all of that was from North Carolina. Of North Carolina's production, much of it centered on the woodlands around our local creeks. Tar kilns and turpentine distilleries were common features in local woods as a way to make money from pine barrens that were otherwise unproductive.

Read this and be amazed: In 1840, Craven County alone produced 139,000 barrels of tar, pitch, turpentine and rosin, about one-fourth the production of the entire United States of America. At 31½ gallons to the barrel, that is 4,378,000 gallons. At 320 pounds to the barrel, 44,480,000 pounds of naval stores were shipped from here that year. The local products were exported worldwide. They were in high demand, especially to England with its large navy and shipbuilding industry.

One of the ways all this material was transported was by "rafting" the barrels from a landing on shore out to the anchorage of one of the ships that routinely ran the Neuse River route. A signal flag would be raised on shore and the ship's captain would know there was product to come aboard. Barrels were lashed together and rowed to the waiting ship where the crew raised them on board with block and tackle.

The resin extraction process could be hard on the trees and eventually led to declines in production. Local resident Hardy Loftin Jones came up with an improved extraction method said to extend the economic life of the tree and applied for a patent in 1843.

"Gathering turpentine," as the industry was known, was big business. Following local combat during the Civil War, the seizure from one location of 1,000 barrels of turpentine was reported. Wills going back to colonial times are preserved at the Craven County courthouse. One estate inventory from the period around the Civil War lists 29 barrels of turpentine and two copper stills. The copper turpentine stills had capacities of 70 to 180 gallons and were valued at $1,500 to $2,000, a particularly hefty sum in those days. The copper still had been introduced in the 1830s. It quickly created a tremendous boost in volume allowing the production of huge quantities of turpentine.

To make tar, pine logs were piled up and covered with earth in a beehive-shaped mound about five to eight feet high and, say, 15 to 45 feet in diameter. Deadwood from fallen trees could also be used, as well as limbs, roots, stumps, and knots. The wood was set on fire and as it burned slowly over several days the tar oozed out into a trench dug beneath the pile. From there it was ladled into buckets and barrels. What was left of the wood after the process was charcoal, which could be used for heating, cooking and foundry work. Though primitive, this was a highly profitable business because of its low cost. When a team of archaeologists surveyed Cherry Point in recent decades, they found the earth literally pockmarked with tar kiln sites.

Tar, used to coat and preserve wood, was processed to make creosote and boiled or "burned" to create pitch. The shiny, sticky wood tar pitch was used primarily for caulking seams to prevent leaks. Rosin is a by-product of turpentine distillation and was used to make varnish.

Business boomed. A number of gristmills and sawmills operated here. The railroad was completed to the hamlet in 1858 and served the naval stores and woodland industries business. Much of the timber shipped from Havelock Station was also used for shipbuilding. There appears to have been some shipbuilding activity in our own backyard. One of the tributaries near the mouth of Slocum Creek is identified on old maps as "Shipyard Gut."

Up to this period, business thrived and local people prospered. By the time of the War Between the States, however, Havelock was dependent upon an industry on the wane.

The problem was that wooden ships and steam engines were not compatible. Steam engines create huge torque; too much stress for a wooden ship. The constant vibration caused the ships to leak badly. Fire on board was another factor that led to the use of iron in ship construction.

When gold was discovered in California in 1849, San Francisco harbor filled to capacity with sailing vessels abandoned by crews who went off to search for riches. Wooden sailing ships were king. In the mid-1860s, as illustrated by the *Harper's Weekly* engravings, the shipping industry was in transition. Within 20 years following the Civil War, the commercial sailing ship was becoming a thing of the past. Ships with metal hulls plied the oceans of the world and the market for naval stores all but ceased to exist. With it, slowly, went the economy of eastern Craven County.

Some say pine borers hurt local forests and that the trees were overused. Some have suggested the devastation of the war itself and the freeing of the slaves from local plantations in 1862 were major factors. But even if production declined for these reasons, the advent of steam ships marked the bitter end.

Demand collapsed. The tar kilns fires went out. The distilleries gathered dust. Jobs and ready money went away. In this small place, among these few hardy souls descended a localized depression that would last, more or less, until the construction of the Marine air base 75 years after the end of the War Between the States.

Beginning with this collapse, the population of Township Six, roughly from Harlowe to Carolina Pines, would continue to decline for most of the next century. In 1930 the population was 861. By 1940 it had dropped to just 723 people. My conclusion after years of consideration is that there may have been more people here in 1835 than there were in 1935.

The early settlers, hit by hard times, moved away, one by one. Most could not sell their land. There was no one to buy it. They just packed up and went. Those who chose to stay behind can be described by one word: poor. One historian described the local populace after this time as "transient." People came and went. Mostly they went.

To illustrate, we can follow a chain of real estate transactions beginning with a 200-acre land grant on what is now Cherry Point to William Stewart in 1757. Three years later, Stewart sold the land to the widow Mary Thompson. She sold the property in 1767 to Jacob Harrington who sold it in 1771 to George Perkins. Perkins sold it in 1774 to John Howard. Howard kept the property 26 years before selling it to Isaac Perkins in 1801. Twenty-nine years later, in 1830, the land was conveyed to William, Martin, and George Carter. The brothers bought the land—a "hot property" for more than 70 years—in the middle of the naval stores boom.

Then, silence.

There was no further sale, deed or legal activity whatsoever on the land until 1930. That year the federal government and the courts began tax proceedings resulting in foreclosure and seizure by the United States of America. Sometime in the intervening years, the Carters, like many others, walked away from their land.

In 1939, the federal government instituted condemnation lawsuits to take the land where the Cherry Point Marine Corps Air Station is today. At the time there were 42 farms there. Forty-two farms would suggest 42 owners, more or less. Counting spouses, it could be no more than 84 owners. In fact, one suit alone named more than 700 individuals as defendants. Some of them had been dead and gone more than 100 years.

The Slocumbs, here since 1702, went to Wayne County, near Goldsboro, and then farther south. The Always and some of the Hancocks went to Kentucky. One branch of the Hancocks went "down east." The Holtons went to Pamlico. Some people moved to find work in New Bern and beyond. Some can be traced to Alabama, Georgia and Tennessee. Many went west. Most of the local names from the rosters at the beginning of the book just vanished.

And there were other names unaccounted for. Take these few, for example, all neighbors here in a single year, 1707. Alexander Goodgroom had 220 acres of land on Handcock's Creek. Near Goodgroom lived Dutton Lane and Bryant Lee. Edward Beicheino owned land on Slocumb's Creek next to Robert Coleman's 250 acres and not too far from the property of Dennis O'Dyar. Another neighbor was Edward Haynes with 640 acres on Handcock's Creek. In a transaction recorded at the Craven County courthouse, Amy Thirel sold 300 acres on the same creek to John Clark.

What became of the Goodgrooms, the Thirels, the Beicheinos and many others are tales dimmed by the mist of history.

One of these stories belongs to the oddly named Physioc family.

5

A Visit to the Old Homeplace

*J*ust before Christmas, 1987, I called Martha Physioc Larson on the telephone. I had read an article she had written about her ancestors who settled in the Havelock area in 1734. In that year North Carolina was still a British colony being ruled by imperial bureaucrats from the capital in New Bern. Mrs. Larson's article indicated that, some 250 years before, John Physioc moved his wife and four children here from Cecil County, Maryland. He called himself a planter, but he may have worked in the beginning with a well-known colonial surveyor named John Lovick. Physioc (pronounced FIZ-ee-ahk) was "pretty well off" and, upon his death, left substantial land holdings for his children, Peter, Rebecca Austin, Charles, and Sydney.

According to her article—Number 410 in the Craven County Heritage Book—Mrs. Larson knew most of the family tree which spanned many generations. She knew who married whom. She knew stories about the family, like the time the big, husky Physioc men held some voters in a field all day so they could win an election. But she had never been able to discover where the family's land and home had been.

Through a curious set of circumstances, I told her on the phone, I knew where it was.

One of the personal interest projects I completed over several years in the early 1980s was a local cemetery survey. There are old cemeteries all over the place around here from single graves to more than 100. There are 17 on Cherry Point alone. One of the oldest cemeteries, the eternal resting place of two of our earliest settlers, Evan and Sally Jones, was moved to make way for the Number One tee box of the Cherry Point golf course.

Actually, the federal government took good care of the burial grounds on the Marine Corps base. They did find it necessary to move some graves, but they recorded headstone information, surveyed and made maps of the layouts, and protected all of them with demarcation fencing, usually metals bollards with wire cable running around the cemetery perimeter.

The Physiocs, however, were not on Cherry Point.

Some years before, on an old map of the Croatan National Forest, I had seen a little square with a cross in it. A church, I suspected, but no, the key indicated that was the symbol for a cemetery. According to what I could determine, the cemetery was marked on the map because it had been the site of a project by either the Civilian Conservation Corps (C.C.C.) or the Works Progress Administration (W.P.A.) during the Great Depression.

In the financial calamity that began with the great stock market meltdown in 1929, the U.S. government put unemployed folks, men mostly, to work doing all kinds of projects. Sending the unemployed to camps around the country shortened the soup lines in the big cities and accomplished much "public work." That was when the Blue Ridge Parkway was built, for example. There had been a C.C.C. camp near Central Highway No. 10, now called U.S. 70, just off what is now Slocum Road,

Cherry Point's western entrance. Many of the men were set to work planting trees in the new Croatan National Forest.

In the first 25 years of the century, Roper Lumber Company, the largest such company in the South, had clear-cut most of the forest. Following the mammoth timber operation, the land was purchased by the federal government for the creation of what would become the 156,000-acre national forest. One of the first things that had to be done was tree planting. Along with planting pines, the C.C.C. workers did surveying and mapping, built forestry roads and campgrounds, erected fire towers and worked on drainage. When they were discovered, the men would also clean up old, overgrown burying grounds.

A short time after seeing the map, I was on Cahooque Creek Road, (pronounced CAH-hookey) down Highway 101 a few miles from Havelock, looking for the cemetery site. Here are hundreds of acres of national forest land along the dirt road leading to a State Wildlife boat ramp. There were no markers to show the way. I could only guess where it might be. I spent some time getting nowhere. A local resident assured me that there was no cemetery around those parts. He had hunted those woods all his life, he said, and had "never seen no cemetery."

The map, however, did have contour lines and the square with the cross was at the head of a certain ravine containing a small creek south of the boat landing. I walked carefully along Hancock Creek, counted the appropriate number of ravines and began to walk straight into it. After a gradual rise of about 100 yards at the end of the ravine, on a pretty wooded knoll, was the loveliest little cemetery you ever saw.

This is a big payoff in the life of a historian, amateur or not. You are tempted to shout, "Eureka!" or something equally as silly.

The thick snow-white marble headstones stood about three feet tall and resembled little headboards for a bed. They were exquisitely carved; obviously the headstones of the well-to-do. One marker announced the grave of

Joseph Physioc
born circa 1786
died Oct. 27, 1841
Aged 58 years, one month and 24 days

The matching marker listed

Eliza Hope Physioc
born circa 1789
died April 1, 1839

There were several unmarked depressions indicating other graves.

The cemetery itself was fenced and though leaf-covered was in otherwise good shape. What struck me most was the strange last name, a name I had never seen anywhere.

Now, years later, on the Sunday after my phone call, my children and I accompanied Martha Physioc Larson, aged 76, into the woods off Cahooque Creek Road. She and her sister, Elinor Physioc Fletcher, had searched for the family roots for many years.

Joseph Physioc, she told me, was one of the six children of Peter, who was the son of the original settler, John. All of the Physiocs were land owners, businessmen and civic leaders. They had substantial land holdings that I would later learn included property on both sides of Hancock Creek. She was a direct descendent of these pioneers.

The cemetery before us confirmed that now, at long last, she was standing on the grounds of the old Physioc homeplace.

As prosperous as the Physiocs had been, they too pulled up stakes and left during the local Depression of the late 1800s. Some Physiocs found their way to West Virginia. Some made it all the way to Kansas. Their land here was abandoned, unsold. In 1939 the federal courts began condemnation of the land where Cherry Point is today. Along with those of many other missing pioneers, the names John, Joseph, Peter, and William Physioc appeared on the list of "defendants" whose land was claimed by the base.

But Mrs. Larson did not care about that. In some small way, she had made a connection with the past, with family long gone. In some small way she had come home. We stayed about an hour, quiet at times, walking and looking. We talked and took photographs.

When we were leaving, with tears in her eyes, she touched my arm and said, "This is the best Christmas present I could have received."

Me, too, Mrs. Larson. Me, too.

6

The Moon Shines on Havelock

*O*kay, so it's 1882 and you're broke.

The naval stores industry, a major cash cow for 150 years, has gone bust. All the neighbors, except a few, have moved away. Land ain't worth a darn for farming. You are stuck here, man, stuck in the pine forests of eastern Craven County with a woodlands lifestyle and a distillation technology.

What are you going to do?

Hmmm? Let me think. Cocktails, anyone?

All those stories you have heard about Havelock and Harlowe and moonshine, well, they are all true and then some.

More than a few local fortunes are based on the copper coil. Many of the descendents are alive and know that Daddy and Momma used to sell Mason jars of clear, strong liquid right out of the house. One home, still visible on Highway 70, was set up so you could pull your ol' pickup right up to the kitchen window and buy yourself a quart. That's right, a moonshine drive-through.

You want to know who was involved in the production of local booze during the big Prohibition heyday and after? The hint I have been given about the Big Names is to look at local street signs. Many of the older street names in Havelock are reputed to have an odd coincidence with the names of local moonshiners.

The reader will have to guess which they are because I am not going to name names. I will use first names and nicknames and aliases. But I stick to my promise; every word is true as it was rendered to me.

Corn liquor was made here from the very beginning.

In colonial times, it was just being sociable to entertain neighbors and wayfaring travelers. The soldiers in the War Between the States commented on the local supply. They called it "chain lightning." But after the collapse of the naval stores industry, after the big "out-migration," the business really took off and it flourished through the years of federal Prohibition (1920-1933) when a local brand gained national recognition and kept right on going until the 1950s when the Marine Corps loaned its helicopters to local revenuers to find still sites from the air.

When I was in high school here in the 1960s, I worked as a stock clerk and cashier at a grocery, the Colonial Store, in the Slocum Shopping Center on Park Lane. Every Friday afternoon, like clockwork, a tall slender black man came into the store and bought two fifty-pound bags of Dixie Crystals sugar and two cases of Falstaff beer. This was the legal limit of both. In fact, the only reason we stocked 50-pound bags of sugar was this guy. Maybe he drank 6.85 beers a day or entertained a lot. But the sugar? Now, certainly, sugar is a main ingredient in the production of moonshine, but I figure they just ate a lot of breakfast cereal around that household. Wink, wink.

A still was discovered after it started a woods fire and was blown up by the sheriff in Harlowe in the early 1990s. There is an even chance that somebody around these parts is cooking up a batch right now.

One historian put it this way: "After the Civil War [1861-1865] lumber became the area's chief industry, staffed by a transient population. The long-term residents were mostly subsistence farmers. One of the major farm industries was the production of illegal corn whiskey, and Harlowe, a community east of Havelock, acquired a reputation as eastern North Carolina's moonshine capital. Havelock follows close behind."

A subsistence farmer is a person who grows just enough to stay alive. He and his family eat what they raise and have little else to show for it. They live, as the expression goes, "hand to mouth." As noted before, the hamlet was economically depressed and the people were poor. Many families were impoverished and destitute. The reason the people of Havelock and Harlowe made and sold moonshine whiskey, a brand that became known far and wide as Craven County Corn, or CCC for short, was to stay alive, to keep a roof over their heads and shirts on their backs. It was a difficult and harsh life. These were hard times, some of the hardest this country has seen.

So despite the inherent Hee-Haw hillbilly hilarity of the idea of moonshinin', it is important to note and remember that these were actually industrious people who worked hard to make some money simply to survive.

Drawing on old newspaper accounts, one writer, Reuel Henry Pietz, said that "the attempts by authorities to stop the practice of illegal liquor manufacture [in Havelock] helped develop a close-knit community, distrustful of strangers and making them loyal to their own people, even though they did not all agree that whisky-making was proper. Local people were assumed to be good and outsiders were believed to be bad."

Some folks actually managed to become prosperous through the years. They were able to buy land, farm equipment and livestock. As time went by they bought vehicles and other niceties. But mostly these were hardscrabble people just trying to keep body and soul together.

Take the true story of the two Freds. One was black, one was white. White Fred lived on what is now Roosevelt Boulevard not too far inside the main gate of the Cherry Point Marine Corps Air Station. At the time, of course, there was no base. It was just farm and woodlands on a dirt road leading from Havelock to Cherry Point Landing where the Hancock boat docks are today.

White Fred, a family man with lots of relatives nearby, listed himself on Craven County tax records as a "farmer." Those same tax records, however, indicate that Farmer Fred owned exactly one acre of land. How much farming do you think he could do on a single acre? Fred did something else to earn his daily bread. He made, transported and sold white lightnin'. White Fred, some say, liked to sample his own product, maybe a little too much. Sometimes he liked drinking it more than making it. But he got by.

Then there was Black Fred. Black Fred was a neighbor of White Fred living less than half a mile away on a farm located where Cherry Point runways are today. Black Fred did have a substantial farm and through the years accumulated more land. Black Fred had enough land to grow his own corn, a handy benefit.

You have probably guessed that Black Fred's corn did not land on any dinner plate. Nope, Black Fred, too, was a bootlegger and quite a good one. In fact, Black Fred, a family man, too, became one of the most prosperous citizens around. On his farm he lived in a two-story house, possibly the nicest of the 42 farm houses that once dotted the local land.

He had substantial outbuildings: barns, a smokehouse, garage, and workshop. He had a Model A Ford pickup truck and a car. This was quite a spread in the midst of the Great Depression.

Without the sale of corn liquor the two Freds would have had little to nothing and would have had a hard time getting even that.

7

Revenuers

The Mason Becton story below was told to me as fact. I have changed the name of the hero and jazzed it up a little, but the person who told me this swore every word was the gospel truth.

*R*evenuers.

That's what they called the state and federal agents from Raleigh and other outlandish places who would ply the dirt roads to eastern Craven County during Prohibition in search of moonshiners. Havelock and Harlowe were prime destinations. They were the undisputed home of Craven County corn liquor, known as "CCC," transported by fast cars, trucks, trains, barges and boats, and famous up the entire East Coast, all the way to Canada.

Pure. Cheap. Effective. CCC. Praised as nectar of the gods. Cursed as the poison of Satan. CCC. Sold by the cup, the pint, the quart jar or by the barrel.

Everyone around these parts was on the lookout for the agents. After all, they could send you or a friend or a relative to prison for a long time. The consequences were serious. In the United States in 1932 there were 80,000 Prohibition convictions. Not just arrests, but convictions. A guilty verdict on charges of manufacture, sale or distribution of illegal liquor could and did result in confinement in the Federal Penitentiary in Atlanta.

Federal prohibition of the manufacture, sale or transportation of alcohol began with the passage of the 18th Amendment in 1919 and ended with the passage of the 21st in 1933. North Carolina being North Carolina had prohibited all that 10 years earlier and never did vote to repeal the 18th Amendment. So while bootleggers nationwide had 13 years to ply their trade, North Carolina distillers had an entire generation.

It is said that the first thing most of the agents did upon arrival, after a long hot dusty drive, was stop at one of the local stores for something cool to drink or to use the outhouse. Invariably this would result in someone going out the backdoor to race down the creeks sounding the alarm for folks to be on the lookout. One female shopkeeper with a store along the highway had quite a reputation for spotting this form of trouble and getting the word to her friends and relations.

Revenuers used spies. They sometimes worked undercover. There were local lawmen, some of whom turned a blind eye, but others who took the oath or personal grudges seriously.

One story is told of a man who worked for his moonshiner brother-in-law, but then had the great good fortune of being hired as a deputy sheriff. A government job in those lean days was manna from heaven. It was hard to get, hard to keep, but guaranteed family survival. The day after walking off the still site in the woods near Gray Road, the brand new deputy came back to arrest his brother-in-law. The brother-in-law's leg was broken in the fight that ensued, but he did, indeed, go to jail.

Some of the time, lawmen posed as travelers or sportsmen. Teeming with bears, deer, rabbits, quail, dove, ducks and alligators, the woods and creeks and river here were widely known to be prime places for hunting and fishing. People, some of them rich or famous or both, came from Raleigh, Durham, Greensboro, Kinston, and as far away as New York City to partake of nature's bounty. The fact that there was pretty good booze and a few bawdy houses did not hurt attendance any either.

One particular day, Miss Xenia Becton's brother, Mason, a renowned distiller of fine spirits, stood on the dirt track known since colonial times as the Beaufort Road. Today it is called Highway 101 and, more precisely, Fontana Boulevard. If you want to be exact about it, he was at the point that is now marked by Gate Six to the Cherry Point Marine Corps Air Station, the gate where Cunningham Boulevard points toward City Hall. A half-mile away the Wynne family had a big hog wallow known today as Havelock City Park. Of course, on that day in 1931, the City of Havelock did not exist and the Marine Corps was a decade away from this distant, rural, backwoods portion of North Carolina.

The settlement called Havelock at the time was closer to Nine Mile Road, now known as Lake Road. It straddled the junction of the railroad tracks with Central Highway No. 10, later called U.S. 70, now called Miller Boulevard, around the locale of Trader's Store.

So when the revenuers approached Mason they were on a narrow, sandy road, surrounded by forest, pretty much in the middle of nowhere.

Mason was a black man, middle-aged, short, balding, and well built. It was a warm day but he wore his "Sunday-go-to-meeting" clothes anyway: a full suit with vest; pocket watch chain shining in the sun. A shoe box, bound with string, was under his arm. Mason had been waiting on a ride down 101 to his home at Little Witness.

Little Witness, for those who do not know, was a black settlement on the north side of the Beaufort Road at its first curve outside of Havelock. Today, it is behind the chain link fence of the Marine base. At that time, though, Little Witness was quite a place with a church, a school, a cemetery or two, and streets with names, even if they were dirt. Little Witness disappeared forever just after 1940 when federal land agents condemned the place, along with other base land, paying about $13 dollars an acre.

Mason's ride had not arrived when the revenuers showed up. The black Ford pulled to a stop within a few feet of him.

"Hey old man," the driver said. "Know where we can get a little something to drink?"

Mason said, "Whatcha lookin' for?"

The driver said they'd like maybe a quart of the "good stuff."

Mason said, "No, sir." They asked again. They said they were down to "do a little fishing" and just wanted a little drink to pass the time. Mason kept telling the strangers that he did not know how to help them.

They begged and pleaded and cajoled, acting down right desperate for a drink. Mason, despite suspecting they might be lawmen, finally began to relent, saying maybe he did know someone who could help. He was telling the revenuers that he knew a man who might have some squeezins' when another vehicle, this one a ramshackle flat bed truck, pulled up at the intersection.

Polite as can be, Mason said he had to go, but the revenuers insisted they had a powerful thirst and beseeched him in desperate terms to help them out. Popular wisdom said almost everybody around Havelock, black or white, was a bootlegger, or at least knew one, and, like all state agents, they had come to make a name for themselves by taking down liquor law violators. The old man hesitated and then told them, reluctantly, to give him some money and he would come back shortly with some "peach brandy" that he was sure they would like.

The driver consulted with his partner for a moment and then asked a question.

"If I give you the money, how do I know you'll come back?"

Mason scratched his chin and then suggested that the gentleman hold his shoes until he returned.

That seemed fair enough. The revenuers forked over the requested number of dollar bills and Mason handed the shoebox into the window of the Ford.

"Be back shortly," he said, walking to the dusty pickup. He climbed in the old truck, gears scraped, and it raised a cloud as it headed down the Beaufort Road toward Harlowe and then on out of sight.

The young revenuers sat smug and excited expecting that in a short time they would make an arrest and carry their prisoner back to New Bern for booking. The one on the passenger side checked his pistol, clicking open the cylinder, as if the bullets might have evaporated. The slugs were still there.

The pair couldn't believe their luck. They'd only been in Hooterville for a few minutes and already they were going to put a moonshiner away.

Fifteen minutes passed. It was hot in the sun. At a half hour, they began to wonder what was taking so long.

Forty-five minutes after Mason rode away in the flatbed truck, the lead agent behind the wheel of the state-owned Ford picked up the shoebox, gave it a shake and began to pull on the twine that bound it shut.

He lifted the lid of the shoebox, pushed aside wads of newspaper and took a deep breath. There were no shoes inside.

In the shoebox, though, was a glass fruit jar with a screw-on lid. Inside the jar, a few peach halves floated gracefully in a quart of genuine, crystal clear, pure, top quality Craven County corn liquor.

8
Local Railroad Tales

*C*raven County Corn, our very own famous "CCC," went all over the East Coast. One method of transport was the railroad that passed through Havelock on a daily basis. The eastern terminus of the line was the Port of Morehead City, a route that led to ships that plied the entire Atlantic seaboard. To the west, the train could carry freight anywhere.

Cherry Trader Roycraft's father, Hugh Trader, was the proprietor of Trader's Store. The now closed, but recently restored landmark, sits where it has long sat, just a stone's throw from the railroad tracks. In a 1976 interview, Cherry explained what her father told her about the transport of the local corn derivative.

"Dad used to say that most of the illegal liquor left Havelock via the train," she said. "They would bring carloads of potatoes up from Beaufort and sometimes a loaded car would be sidetracked overnight. Those moonshiners took their jars of corn and hid them among the potatoes and when the train picked up the abandoned carload and took their cargo to New Bern and northward, they carried the stowaway bottles, too."

The train was handy for other things as well. Before the expansion of the rail line to our neck of the woods, foot or horse travel was most common; then it was a half-day's journey to New Bern and another half-day back. A primary means of travel was by water. Boats, especially canoes, were common. More than one local family owned a sailboat. Boats, though, were not much faster than walking. On the train you could make the trip, with no effort, in an hour. Or you could send a list of supplies to New Bern and get your goods back, possibly the next day.

The opening of the rail line here had an impact hard to imagine. Its effects simply cannot be overstated. Changes wrought by the Internet and the space shuttle pale in comparison to the train's arrival in Havelock.

The Weekly Union, a newspaper published in New Bern, announced on June 3, 1858, "We have learned that the last rail of the Atlantic and N. C. Railroad was laid Monday."

The completion came 23 years after the construction of the rail line was first authorized by the N. C. General Assembly. It was quite a relief. For years, the newspapers were filled with angry sniping, recrimination, blame and broken promises regarding the failure to get the job done. Very much like the current Havelock bypass.

A June 12, 1858, newspaper article declared, "The first train from Goldsboro to Morehead City [ran on] Monday, June 7, 1858. The train was composed of two passenger cars filled to their utmost capacity with politicians, pleasure seekers, and not a few members of the fairer sex from New Bern, Kinston, etc. who left the depot for Morehead City." This was the first train to cross Slocum's Creek and the old Beaufort Road, at the place we now call Havelock.

It was an inauspicious start as the two candidates for governor held a debate in Beaufort that night at which a fist fight broke out. The newspaper article alleged, "Judge E dealt Mr. M a blow that was quickly returned." Another article said the dispute was "amicably settled."

We do not know who won the fight but Judge E, also known as John W. Ellis, a Democrat from Rowan County, won the governorship. Ellis died in office during the civil war that would soon follow.

To give some perspective on the era, in that same issue of the paper were headlines reading: *Bloody battle between Texas Rangers and Comanche Indians; Yellow fever in New Orleans;* and *Progress on the submarine telegraph cable across the Atlantic*

The Atlantic and North Carolina Railroad became known as the "Old Mullet Road" or "Old Mullet Line" due to the large quantities of fish and other seafood hauled up the tracks from Morehead City.

Interestingly, and despite what has previously been written, to date I have found no reference to a railroad depot from this period. While the place is called Havelock Station, no newspaper article, map, or military record mentions a depot or railroad building of any kind.

There are three possibilities to explain this:

1) A depot was built here in 1857 and named Havelock Station and nobody wrote much about it or I just haven't found it yet. Quite possible.

2) A depot was built here in 1857 and named Havelock Station and it was destroyed at the very beginning of the War of Northern Aggression. I do not think so.

3) No depot was built at the time. "Havelock Station" referred to the place, the crossroad, possibly a point of re-supply for firewood and water. A station can be a building, but it can also be a place. I believe this to be correct.

We will talk more about the number, dates and location of Havelock train depots later.

One of the first actions of the Civil War involved the railroad at Havelock. This poignant piece entitled *A Remembrance* was published in a Goldsboro newspaper in 1909. In it the writer, J. M. Hollowell, recalls the beginning of the war.

"On the 13th of April, 1861, the town [of Goldsboro] was full of country people who with the citizens of the town kept close to the telegraph office for news of the firing that was going on upon Fort Sumter at Charleston, S.C., but at sunset no news of its surrender had been received. The result came sometime after nightfall.

"There was no telegraph line then to New Bern. When the train for that place left on Saturday the 13th at 3 o'clock p.m., the fort was still holding out. That was the latest from there.

"The people of New Bern could not wait until Monday to hear further from Charleston. There being no train on the A. & N.C.R.R. on Sunday, they besought the president, Col. J.D. Whitford, to send an extra engine and coach to Goldsboro, which he did, and it came loaded with the most prominent men of New Bern.

"On Monday morning, Gov. Ellis wired Capt. Craton to proceed with his company [the Goldsboro Rifles] to Fort Macon, and take possession of that fortification. But Capt. Josiah Pender, of Beaufort, N.C., anticipated the Governor's desire and on Sunday, April 14th, with a detachment of men from Beaufort went over to the fort and took possession, there being only one man, Sgt. Alexander, in charge of the place.

"But Capt. Craton began to collect his men. Some of them lived several miles in the country, and by 3 o'clock, when the New Bern train left, he had them aboard."

"Bless you, those were exciting times. The people were stirred as I never saw them before, nor since. That day I saw the first tears of the war, as the wives, parents, sisters, brothers and friends stood at the train to bid the soldier boys goodbye; but alas, the tears that day were but the beginning of the floods of tears that followed in the next four years."

According to Hollowell's report, on April 16, 1861, Confederate forces, the first N.C. troops known as the "Goldsboro Rifles," passed by rail through Havelock. This troop movement came just three days after the fall of Fort Sumter and the day after President Lincoln called for 75,000 troops to suppress the Southern rebellion. Thus, less than three years after the completion of the rail line, Havelock was in the middle of a war.

9

Yanks vs. Rebs

𝒯he Battle of New Bern and the assault on Fort Macon are well documented and often reported. There is little need to re-fight the entire Burnside Campaign here. For those who want all the details, local libraries are awash in the information. We recommend the effort. It is a great story.

For the time being, here is the short version.

After landing at Slocum's Creek on March 13, 1862, the Union force marched up the rail line and old road to New Bern. A few miles this side of the Trent River, in the vicinity of what is now James City, they routed the smaller, less-well-trained, less-well-led Rebel force in a significantly bloody battle. There were numerous acts of gallantry by the Confederate force defending its home, but it was quickly overwhelmed. The surviving Confederates promptly skedaddled on the train to Kinston and beyond, burning their bridges behind them.

For the small forces involved, the casualties were high, at almost 1,100. The most reliable count put the Union dead at 90 with 384 wounded and one missing. The Confederate death toll was 64, with 101 wounded and 413 either missing or captured.

With the Port of New Bern secure, Burnside's raiders moved east and focused a brilliant campaign on re-taking the Rebel-held Fort Macon guarding the mouth of Beaufort harbor. That facet of the expedition is a particularly good read.

Once Fort Macon fell, for all intents and purposes, the "Civil War" was over in this part of eastern North Carolina. So from 1862-1865, the devastation that was poured on much of the rest of the Southern states was diminished here. Oh, there were a couple of half-hearted attempts by the South to retake the place, but nothing happened. The Yankees were set up very well in New Bern. They held what there was of Morehead City at the time. They held Beaufort and everything in between. The slaves were freed. Except for an occasional skirmish, fighting ceased. There was plenty of devastation nonetheless and plenty of hardship for the locals. It took about 100 years to get over it.

What we can add to this well-known story are some details we think are unreported locally; the observations of a young Union captain who landed at Slocum's Creek as part of General Ambrose E. Burnside's invasion force, saw duty at New Bern and Fort Macon, and made a memorable trip to Havelock Station.

His name was Levi Kent.

Capt. Levi E. Kent served with Company F of the 4th Rhode Island Infantry Regiment. In his journal, Capt. Kent, provides us with an invaluable tool for understanding the conflict that may be the single most important local historical event.

While some of what we repeat here focuses on New Bern, it must be remembered that the Yankee invasion disrupted life for everyone in Havelock, which was occupied from 1862-1865, the remainder of the war. The battle itself, a sharp, bloody event, was fought between Havelock and New Bern, up and down the Neuse River. Kent was in the thick of the fight.

I came across Kent's journal last year. It is now housed and owned by the William L. Clements Library at the University of Michigan, Ann Arbor. There is no copy in print. The portion used here was transcribed from the original.

Kent kept a journal during his service in the war from 1861 to 1862. He made entries daily and sometimes twice daily. He was a good, descriptive writer. From time to time, there were periods of a few days when no entry was made. Usually this was because he had been in action with his unit.

The young Kent was both homesick and ill with a stomach ailment through much of the campaign. There was, however, an air of excitement in his entry of March 12, 1862. From his ship, the steamer Eastern Queen anchored in Albemarle Sound, Kent wrote that the weather was "splendid" and everyone was "in good humor." He said there were "signs of preparation for our starting throughout the fleet."

There had been a "rumer," he noted in his unique spelling, that "Newberne & Norfolk" might be the object of the operation. He also noted that his friend, Capt. Tillinghart, had received a letter from New York informing him of the death of his brother on yet another battlefield. Within a few days the Tillinghart family would be sent the news that another son, the young captain himself, had fallen in the fight for New Bern.

There is no entry in the journal from March 12, the day the Burnside fleet arrived off Slocum's Creek, until Kent penned the following four days after the Battle of New Bern. Writing from "Rebel Camp Lee," a former Confederate campground "near Newberne, N.C.," Kent said, "Our little Army has again made its mark and routed the rebels from a position they considered secure."

In other words, Capt. Kent and the rest of Burnside's force had won the Battle of New Bern. His outfit had now made itself comfortable in a rebel camp that was all set up and ready for occupancy after the Confederates abandoned it following the battle. Kent, among other things, was in charge of the Color Guard, the soldiers who carried, displayed, and protected the force's flags.

"On the night of the 12th we laid at anchor just above Slocoms Creek in the Neuse River," he wrote. "On the morning of the 13th the force was landed at the mouth of Slocoms Creek by the light draft Steamers & Launches and a march commenced toward Newberne."

After moving as close to shore as possible, he and his men jumped into the water and waded ashore. Their landing was in a stand of tall, thick marsh grass. Once ashore they planted the Stars and Stripes as a rallying point for the other disembarking troops. Soon, he said, they were in line and marching toward New Bern.

They marched "all that day, at times weary and tiresome." It rained all day, sometimes heavily. Their first halt for rest was near a deserted farm house between the landing site and Croatan. Kent said "the occupants had fled."

"Lieut. Greene & I paid the house a visit," he said. "The troops before us had turned every thing upside down. The furniture once nice was a complete wreck. A piano was being pumped to its utmost & was sadly bruised. Some few articles of food were left to which the boys helped themselves & somebody brought Greene & myself some pickles that were good."

They continued to march through rain and drizzle looking for Confederate resistance. At about four in the afternoon they reached "quite an extended earthwork of the enemy, which covered the

Rail Road (R.R.), the country road, and terminated in quite a formidable earth fort upon the bank of the Neuse."

The first Confederate earthwork was at Croatan and had been deserted by the Confederates shortly before the Union forces arrived. Several earthwork forts lay between Slocum's Creek and New Bern. Kent noted that "no guns were in position except at the River but probably in a few days this extension work would have been in shape to have given us great trouble & held us in check for awhile."

After moving through these massive unoccupied earthworks, they rested for about a half-hour in a grove of pines. Kent was tired and hoped they were stopping for the night, but soon they were marching again. They kept moving along the approximate route of today's U.S. 70 toward New Bern until dark "when our advance came up on the rebel pickets."

At dawn on March 14, the day of the Battle of New Bern, Kent woke up cold and soaked to the bone. It had rained all night.

"Lieut. Greene & myself 'slept together' between two logs," the captain wrote. "We slept upon my Blanket covering us with his. We were completely soaked & the water [rose] to three inches deep where we lay. The camp fires had blazed away all night and many probably less tired had sat about them."

Within minutes, the force was on the move. Before long they were approaching Fort Thompson, the earthworks stronghold where the rebels would make their stand. Kent soon found himself "in front of another line of rebel works in the midst of musketry & cannon."

The fighting had begun.

Fighting at New Bern, March 14, 1862

Edward Ellis Collection

In a long passage, the young captain described the movement of troops, the firing, and the confusion of battle. The Confederates were arrayed along a line blocking the advance to New Bern beyond the railroad and all the way to the river. Kent's group first moved from the main road toward the rail line, passing "very near the center of the enemys line of works."

"I was so completely exhausted that all my movements were sort of mechanical," Kent remembered. "I moved more like a machine than a man & I almost feared the machine would break down. But it Kept up and held together through it all for which I am thankfull."

Moving through some young pine trees they were again fired upon by Confederate marksmen. After assessing their situation they hurried down a grade to the rail line. With part of his force in light woods and part behind the railroad embankment, Kent's colonel had completed his orders. Now they waited for further orders from Gen. John G. Parke, one of Burnside's subordinate commanders.

While they waited, the Confederate flanks were being attacked by forces under the other commanders, Gen. John G. Foster and Gen. Jesse Lee Reno. Kent observed that the forces in the Confederate center were withdrawn to support the two ends of the line under attack. "The enemy had withdrawn everything from his centre," Kent said. "This was our fortune."

The collapse of the Confederate center, manned by the most inexperienced troops, is noted in all accounts as the major failure of the defense of New Bern. Kent was there when it occurred and witnessed it with his own eyes.

Kent's group now had nothing directly in front of them. They were under fire, but he indicates the musket fire was ineffective, mostly falling short.

"They peppered at us but did not seem to reach us fairly," he said. "What few shots reached us passed well over."

Fierce fighting was then occurring all along the line. Some of it was hand-to-hand. In some places the Union advance was repulsed. One group of 24th Massachusetts soldiers seized a cannon from enemy hands, but was then driven back over the big earthen berm by a Confederate charge. In the rain and smoke, men were falling dead and wounded by the dozens.

Without orders to do so, Kent "joined by Capt. Buff...went up to the Breastwork & digging steps with my sword I mounted it."

Kent "could distinctly see the rebel Colors on my right on the hill & the heads of a few men...their colors [the rebel flag] I could distinctly see planted on the very line of works on which I was standing."

Meanwhile, several other officers had been conferring and decided to charge their portion of the Fort Thompson earthwork. With the order, the men began to roar and yell or, as Kent said, "and up the hill we went with a tiger and a yah!"

The charge startled the Confederate defenders so badly that they stopped fighting and began a hasty retreat.

"The rebels evidently thought bedlam was not only loose but upon them," Kent said. "They did not stay to receive us but their backs & heels were shown instead as they retreated on a double-double quick, through the woods."

In his journal, Kent proudly underlined the following words: The Colors of my Company were the first planted upon the rebel works.

Kent said the fort was now in Union hands from the railroad to the river. On the other side of the railroad, the fighting continued as the rebels fought "obstinately" against Gen. Reno's forces.

Gen. Parke's troopers, including Kent, began regrouping on the top of the fort's hill-like wall. At that moment, Gen. Burnside himself, having witnessed the successful attack, charged up on a horse. He asked the men if they were the 4th Rhode Island Troops. "Being answered in the affirmative said 'I Knew it.' And away he rode to prepare a new job for us," Kent relates.

The fight was far from over. Reno's men were still laboring to dislodge the rebels across the tracks. After 20 minutes rest, Kent's group was ordered to move and assist Reno. As they charged across the railroad tracks they came under intense fire and begin to rush from one pit and berm to another, firing as they went. The movement of new forces to the fray caused the rebel resistance to collapse. Though effective, the charge cost the Union army 20 killed and wounded. This is where Kent's friend, Capt. Tillinghart, was fatally shot.

Kent says the 5th Rhode Island Volunteers now mounted a charge down the railroad near "a sort of Brick yard." They attacked and routed the Confederate riflemen "in their pits that peppered us while we stood on the R.R. before the charge." Here another of Kent's friends, Lt. H.R. Reice, was killed.

The Battle of New Bern was nearing its end.

"The rebels now put for Newburne," Kent said, "and across the River burning the R.R. & highway bridges behind them. On followed our forces, Foster in advance, and the Gunboats followed up the River. With our advance we soon had [General Foster's] entire brigade in the city."

Kent reports that "near the City we found several encampments of the rebels just as they had left them in the morning when they moved down the road to give us battle." In one of these deserted camps, Kent made a temporary home and completed the entry in his journal from which we have just read.

Kent made a final assessment of the Battle of New Bern that is particularly poignant:

"This is our second engagement [Roanoke Island was the first] & far the most severe. I am not anxious for a repetition of the doings of the 14th but wish it might please God to stop the rebels in their career of madness and return peaceably to their homes."

Among the wounded Union officers, Kent reports, "Capt. Bill Chace has a shot through his cheek and Lieut. Curtis of my company, a wound upon his shoulder."

On March 17, Kent went to see New Bern with his fellow officer Lt. Charley Greene.

"It is a pretty little town and must have been a lovely place in time of peace," Kent said. "Several valuable buildings were destroyed by the rebels as they passed through on their flight."

He reports that in New Bern "one of the enterprising Sutlers," the traveling merchants accompanying the Yankee fleet, had opened the Gaston House hotel, renaming it the Union House. The Gaston House was a large three-story brick hotel on South Front Street.

"Its bar is well patronized," he said.

After visiting "places of importance" in the city, he and Green "went down to the wharf and foraged a boat" and found a couple of the recently freed slaves to row it down river "to our good old *Eastern Queen.*" At the ship, they enjoyed a bath, had a "change of under clothing," a lunch of hard tack and then returned to their camp near New Bern.

"We arrived back at rebel 'Camp Lee' about nine ok [o'clock] in the evening after a very pleasant day," he said. "We were soon comfortably snoozing in quarters."

A few days later, assets were being moved toward Fort Macon for the coming battle there. In a flotilla of three small ships, Kent went by steamer to Havelock to begin the march east. There they put out picket guards, sent a company of troops to Havelock Station, and built temporary shelters from pine limbs. Here Kent tells the story in his own words. (My comments are in parentheses).

Sunday March 23rd 1862
Steamer Eastern Queen
River Neuse

Our good Steamer left her anchorage during the forenoon of the 20th Steaming down the River as far as Slocoms Creek where we landed to commence our march. The weather was anything but pleasant when we left our anchorage in the Neuse and before reaching Slocoms Creek we were having quite a storm again.

The Right Wing of the Regiment goes on board the *Union*; the little stern-wheeler that has attended us so constantly, and preceded by the little Gun boat *Picket* & followed by the Side wheel Steamer *Alice Price*, all small vessels, we commence, we steamed away up (Slocum's) Creek. After picking our tortuous winding for about two miles up the creek we made a landing. At the spot where we landed the Creek was not of sufficient width to turn the *Union* round in.

(The point would be near the current location of Graham A. Barden Elementary School where the creek splits into its two prongs).

After a successful landing and throwing out of pickets, preparations were made for a comfortable bivouac.

Capt. Brown was sent with his company to occupy the R.R. Depot (Havelock Station) about 3/4 of a mile from us.

We built bough huts to keep the rain off & tried to be comfortable.

Before dark the *Union* worked herself out of the grass and returned to the mouth of the River or Creek for the rest of the Regiment.

By the end of the month, the Union was preparing to attack Fort Macon and Kent was living in a tent camp at "Carolina City, N.C." near where Carteret General Hospital in Morehead City is today. On Monday, March 30, he arrived in Havelock by rail on a "train" pulled by mules since the railroad locomotives were otherwise occupied.

With a group of 10 men, Kent accompanied the quartermaster to Havelock Station to pick up tents and stores. Their train was composed of one boxcar and one flatcar drawn by six mules.

Kent had started for Havelock about 9:30 a.m. He said that "10 or 12 miles at mule pace" brought them to Newport "well tired of snail traveling, although some parts of the trip was very pleasant." He said the men in the boxcar were quite happy and that while riding on the flatcar in the sun he had found the trip "very pleasant indeed." It rained, but at Newport they got "some hot drink with a little liquor infused and it did us good."

Five miles outside of Newport they came upon a locomotive-powered "siege train" headed with supplies for the operation against Fort Macon. They had no choice but to backtrack to the Newport side switch and let the other train pass. They arrived at Havelock after dark.

A Lt. Johnson was in charge of the camp at Havelock Station. There was a detail guarding the supplies and luggage Kent had come to pick up. After a tasty dinner of coffee and hardtack, the dry, tough, ever-lasting wafers of unleavened bread that was standard fare, they settled into their tents for the night.

The next morning Kent and another soldier went to find a few more mules. The train would be loaded on the return trip and they needed more pulling power. On horseback they rode about 1½ miles and came upon a "once prosperous plantation with negro accommodations for about one hundred & fifty head of slaves." It is interesting to speculate where this plantation might have been. It could have been the stated distance down Lake Road or toward New Bern or Morehead or Greenfield Heights.

Kent said the plantation owner had left "for parts unknown" as the Union advanced. With him he took his best men "leaving the old & infirm & many very young lasses and a couple of bright looking blacks about twenty-five year old in charge."

"I went into one of plain board cottages," Kent said, "where I saw a fine looking old negress and arranged with her to give us a breakfast. She prepared us some Bacon & eggs & coffee & a johnny cake."

Johnny cake is the Union soldiers' name for a flat cake of cornmeal baked on a griddle.

"Aunty's quarters consisted of but one room," Kent said. "She had quite a stock of provisions as I saw several Hams and strips of Bacon hanging up on the rafters overhead. Two bright silver quarters we gave the old negress [who] brought out her good wines for us without stint."

Of a herd of 20 mules at the plantation's barn, Kent and his comrade selected four for the return trip. Fearing they would lose the mules, the two young men who had been left in charge of the plantation objected to the Union army taking them. Kent made a firm case that the mules were going with them. He said if they wanted to be sure to get them back, the men should go with them and then bring them home.

"This they concluded to do," Kent said.

With the train load of tents, rations and ammunition, they started the return trip to Carolina City at noon and arrived there at 8:00 p.m.

The Levi E. Kent Journal is a treasure. What you have read here is from portions of three days of entries. The entire journal covers parts of two years. One observer called it a virtual "regimental history."

Capt. Kent went on to participate in the taking of Fort Macon. He made friends with a Confederate soldier named Munson in Beaufort. He saw a wharf there loaded with "cotton, resin & turpentine" ready for transport. Kent eventually shipped out at Beaufort for more challenges in the north. He survived the war and was promoted to major. After one year of honorable service he was discharged in September, 1862. Though his post-war activities are unknown, it is presumed he returned home. His writings are another piece in our understanding of the past.

10

Burning the Fort at Master's Mill

$\mathcal{A}$s noted before, Union general Burnside landed his army of 15,000 near the mouth of Slocum's Creek. The men came ashore at Magnolia Plantation, now called Carolina Pines, on March 13, 1862. Within a week, a force of Yankee soldiers was sent to occupy and defend Havelock Station. There they built a "blockhouse," a good-size log fort, as the centerpiece of the local defenses.

Before the war, the site had been the focal point of local business. It was where the steam-powered railroad train stopped for water and fuel. Nearby goods were loaded and unloaded and passengers came and went. A short distance away on the southwest prong of Slocum Creek was a big, busy grist mill that had served the Havelock area for decades. With the approach of war, many Havelock area residents, like the plantation owner in the previous chapter, had fled. Others had gone to join their rebel comrades in the defense of New Bern.

Now the Yankees were here.

Gen. John G. Parke, later in life West Point's superintendent, was in command of the Rhode Island Heavy Artillery under Burnside. According to Parke: "At this time the Third Brigade consisted of three and one-half regiments and the task assigned was to invest Fort Macon and guard the railroad as far north as Havelock Station against the small bands of Confederate cavalry that infested the county to the west."

"On the 19th of March, most of the brigade," Gen. Parke continued, "was ordered to march along the railroad, which it did, reaching Havelock Station...and there bivouacking for the night. The march proved excessively fatiguing to the men, as they had to step from tie to tie on the road bed, and also run hand-cars containing their supplies."

One of the outfits that occupied Havelock Station for a time was the 98th New York Volunteers. During their months encamped by the railroad, they complained bitterly, as is the right of every red-blooded military man. They called Havelock "snake-infested, remote...the worst kind of duty...a crossroads with very few people" and claimed that "the only comfort available is the chain lightning whiskey to be had at every house and store."

One of them wrote in a letter home: "Every locality in that country which contained as much as a blacksmith shop and a store, the principal staple of which was chain lightning whiskey, was dubbed a city and looked upon as a future metropolis."

They also complained about the mud. During the initial invasion, the force encountered one of those week-long rainy spells we know so well. One penned the following bit of verse:

> Now I lay me down to sleep,
> In mud that's many fathoms deep;
> If I'm not here when you awake,
> Just hunt me up with an oyster rake.

According to the History of the Fifth Rhode Island Heavy Artillery, on March 20, 1862, the soldiers were ordered to build a blockhouse at the railroad trestle over Slocum's Creek to "guard it against Confederate cavalry or guerrilla bands that

Union-built blockhouse fort at Havelock Station, 1863

Southern Historical Collection, Wilson Library University of North Carolina at Chapel Hill

might attempt to interdict the route." A hand-drawn Union map from First Division Headquarters, New Bern, N.C., dating from 1862-63 shows the location where these troops built the blockhouse beside the railroad tracks at Havelock.

More troops arrived on March 23. They began cutting timber for the blockhouse fort immediately.

During the fort's construction, a musician with Rhode Island Company B was involved in a "singular accident." The soldier, James McIntyre, was resting under a tree while another tree was being cut down nearby. The tree "suddenly came to the ground, and in some unaccountable manner, a ragged limb of the tree struck Comrade McIntyre near the shoulder, completely pinning him to the ground." The only way he could be extricated "from his perilous position" was by amputation of the arm. He was cared for by Surgeon Potter who "alleviated his suffering."

When the rest of the Union battalion moved out for the Battle of Fort Macon, the history says, "Captain Arnold's Company E was stationed at Havelock, near an abandoned gristmill, the machinery of which the rebels had attempted to destroy when they left that neighborhood. The mechanics of the Fifth...soon put it in running order again, and it was found very serviceable to the comfort and subsistence of the men." The repaired mill allowed the grinding of grain for fresh bread, cornbread, and johnny cakes. For the soldiers, this was a wonderful break from hardtack.

My supposition is that the mill was once owned by Richard Dobbs Spaight (1757-1802), an active patriot, delegate to the Constitutional Convention, and governor of North Carolina, who lived on the south side of the Trent River near New Bern. His plantation spanned thousands of acres. After his death in 1802 it may have been operated by his son of the same name who also served as governor. A remnant of the mill dam is still visible up Slocum Creek from the boat ramp by the Church Road bridge. In operation in 1808, it was then called Spaight's Mill. Like so much else in the pre-Civil War era, it was built with slave labor. The family of Spaight (rhymes with "date") is considered to have been one of Craven County's largest slaveholders.

Spaight owned huge tracts that included much of the land between the Trent River and Havelock, and much of what is modern-day Havelock as well. Some of Spaight's "neighbors" here at Slocumb's Creek included, of course, John and Josiah Slocumb, and also major land owners Frederick Jones, John Hall, Basil Smith, William Winn, Richard Ellis, Thomas Bratcher, and William Wicheliff.

The earthen dam was massive and was capable of holding up to 25 feet of water. The current Coast and Geodetic Survey quadrangle map still lists the circular body of water on the creek there as a mill pond. The dam, with water coming from the creek and via the canal from the lakes near Camp Bryan, would have flooded a huge expanse all the way back to and possibly beyond the railroad trestle.

Such a huge grist milling operation means that the mill would have served a large vicinity's need for the grinding of corn and other grains. This type of water power could also run sawmill equipment. One newspaper article from the 1880s indicates that a commercial sawmill existed there.

The dam was so wide and flat on top that, I have been told, a "tramway" once ran across it. The purpose of a tramway may have been to move wood to and from the sawmill.

There is also a possibility that Spaight sold the land before his death to a member of the Master (sometimes spelled "Masters") family. In 1791, he advertised for sale in the newspaper a tract called "Gamboes" or "the Mill Land." At this writing we are not sure if the advertisement referred to the Slocum's Creek mill or if a sale was consummated. Research continues.

In any event, according to maps, by the 1890s, the place was known as Masters Mill. The name change may have taken place much earlier, but we have a map showing the name in that era. Master is a family name of people who once owned land here and operated the mill after Spaight, 44, was killed in a duel with prominent businessman and political rival John Wright Stanly in New Bern. Thomas Master recorded a deed in 1775, as did Joseph Master in 1791. In that period, Samuel Master is also in the records.

When I was a boy I used to play along the railroad tracks here. My companions and I sometimes spent entire days at the Slocum Creek railroad trestle that is about one-fourth of a mile down the tracks toward New Bern from the current Havelock railroad depot. From Miller Boulevard, it is an easy walk of only a few minutes.

At the time there was a huge round wooden water tank on a wooden tower just like in the movies, the kind with shake shingles on the side. Using water hand-pumped from the creek, the tank would have been used to supply steam locomotives. The stationmaster would have had as one of his responsibilities seeing to it that the tank was kept full of water. By the 1960s, this tank had fallen and was lying in underbrush a few feet from the narrow, deep, rapidly flowing creek. It has since decayed away to nothing.

Beside the creek and nearly on its bank was a brick well rising about three or four feet from the ground. An old brick foundation wall stood on each bank of the creek at the trestle although the railroad trestle itself is now built with big sturdy wooden pilings. There were several more brick foundations along the track, which my childish mind could never decipher.

I am now convinced that this is the site of the original "Havelock Station" of 1858. Probably someone was under contract to cut and deliver wood, which along with the water, was the basic fuel to run the early steam trains. It is easy to imagine this quarter swarming with activity: the big grist mill underway nearby, people at work loading and unloading freight from wagons, barrels of tar and pitch, farm products, and timber, with passengers boarding and the train whistle blowing.

And nearby this site is an earthwork that we called "the Civil War fort." We called it that because kids for generations had called it that. It was a little hill with a commanding view of the railroad trestle although tall trees covered the ground by then. The top of the hill had been dug out making a small depression and around the bottom of the mound was a "firing trench" that encircled the hill.

Here for endless summer hours we fought and re-fought phantom battles against imaginary Yankees, Indian braves and probably a few Nazis along the way.

The "civil war fort" is now on private property off Church Road on Hickory Circle behind the Cherry Point Baptist Church. The site is heavily wooded and is not visible from the road.

There is no doubt that this is the site of the blockhouse, or square log fort enclosure with a roof, built by the Rhode Island Heavy Artillery in 1862. We know from another source that the structure was 1,681 square feet or about as much space as a medium-size single-family home. In addition to its services as a depot, the building and a shanty behind it probably served as "officers' quarters." The enlisted men of the 98th New York Volunteers and others lived for a portion of two years in a tent encampment that filled the vicinity of Woodland Drive behind Cherry Point Baptist.

This location was sketched by Herbert Eugene Valentine, a private from Massachusetts, who served as quartermaster at New Bern military headquarters 1862-1863 and who traveled to the encampment. Valentine's sketch conforms in every way to the lay of the land, even showing the blockhouse on the hillock where I thought the "fort" was as a child. In the drawing he identifies the blockhouse as the "depot" at Slocum Creek. He shows the tent city at the rear of the blockhouse.

Documents in the Southern Historical Collection also refer to a blockhouse at Havelock Station.

So, what happened to the blockhouse depot?

In 1864, on direct orders from General Robert E. Lee, Confederate forces attempted to retake New Bern. The town had fallen into Union hands shortly after Burnside landed in 1862. The attempt failed much to the disgust and aggravation of one R.J. Jeffords, a lieutenant colonel of the 5th South Carolina Cavalry. During the operation, Jeffords sent dispatches to his commanding general.

Excerpts related to the railroad follow in italics:

Feb. 3, 1864
Havelock 12 o'clock
General—I have reached this place. The fort has been deserted. One brass six pounder gun spiked. The fort is now being burnt with quarters. The enemy (one company artillery) left this morning in

the direction of Croatan...troops going toward New Bern.

The fort he mentions is the Union-built blockhouse that had served as the railroad depot at Havelock Station. Quite a battle took place all along the rail line. Retreating troops would often "spike" a cannon they feared might fall into the hands of the enemy by pounding a foreign object, like a spike, into the firing hole. This rendered the cannon useless until a laborious repair was made. Jefford's unit proceeded toward New Bern until the attack failed and he was ordered to retreat. When he sent the following dispatch he was in Jones County.

Feb. 4, 1864
Near White Oak River, 9 p.m.
In obedience to your order I left Croatan at 9 a.m. this day and reached this point via Newport. In my route here I destroyed several road bridges and Railroad bridge and trestle at Havelock...

There is no record suggesting that the Union rebuilt any permanent structure at Havelock following the destruction of the blockhouse and trestle by the retreating Confederate cavalry. The railroad continued to operate under the Union's Quartermaster General until the United States Military Railroad Department took over near the war's end. The tracks and trestle were soon repaired and the Yankees' armored trains resumed their patrol of the Atlantic and North Carolina rail line. The blockhouse fort at Havelock was still in ruin when the war ended in April, 1865.

11

Major Bryan Sells Some Land

The chapter in which we learn that Havelock had at least four general stores in the 1890s.

In 1899, Maj. James Augustus Bryan, a Confederate veteran and wealthy local resident, offered a little land for sale: 57,484 acres to be exact.

The real estate prospectus for the sale of Bryan's property, actually a small booklet, paints the clearest picture of Havelock's turn-of-the-century economic activity so far available. It illustrates commerce with Northern states, as well as local farming, industrial and shipping activity. Details of the Civil War era blockhouse appear in it as well.

A few interesting excerpts follow.

Edward Jack, a Canadian, represented Bryan (born 1839-died 1923) in the sale and authored the prospectus. Writing in 1891 in a section on agricultural wealth he said: "A very large part of Mr. Bryan's tract of 57,484 acres [is] in the vicinity of Havelock station and below New Bern..."

In fact, the land included much of modern-day Havelock and a significant portion of what is now the Croatan National Forest.

In a section on "timber wealth," Jack states that one place he measured the diameter of trees was "on Mr. Bryan's land, close to Havelock, where once stood a blockhouse that was burned in 1865...The size of the mound on which the blockhouse once stood was 41 feet square ...U.S. Troops once camped in the rear of the blockhouse." We know with certainty that the blockhouse burned in 1864. Writing a few decades later, Jack got the date wrong. His other details, however, handily confirm and add to other things we know.

By now Masters Mill is owned by Maj. Bryan. It is sometimes referred to as Bryan's Mill. Jack notes the "excellent water power owned by him [Bryan] at Havelock station, just below the point where Slocum's Creek crosses the line of the A. & N.C. Railway."

In the prospectus, Bryan himself wrote about "the railroad accommodations" at Havelock. "They are easy of access to the Northern cities, to wit: if you leave New York at 9 p.m., you reach Havelock; the station by land, at 7 p.m. the next evening. A telegraph station there would put you in communication with outside points."

"The property controls magnificent water power, consisting of the lakes, which cover an area of 25 square miles of water, with a dam capable of carrying a head of water 25 feet deep. A railroad station [is] within 400 yards of the mill site, which is just 18 miles from the port of New Bern..."

Though seldom seen and little known by most residents, four substantial lakes are within a few miles of Havelock out the appropriately named Lake Road. They are Ellis, Little, Long and Great lakes.

Using slave labor, the lakes were connected to one another by huge canals in the early 1800s and a canal was dug all the way to Slocum Creek near Havelock Station, a distance of five miles. The canals allowed control of the water for irrigation, drainage and to provide water power for the mill site at Slocum Creek. Now within Camp Bryan and the Croatan National Forest, the lakes at the time were on Maj. Bryan's land.

In a section on "hunting advantage" Jack notes: "The lakes are about five miles from Havelock station, on the railway leading from New Bern to Morehead. One can go to the lakes in the morning and return at night, either to Mr. Bryan's farm house, which is three miles from Havelock station, or to the station itself. Mr. Bryan's house, which is surrounded by groves of lofty pine, would be preferable. This place could be a charming sportsman's retreat. The canal which drains the lakes (a rapid stream) passes less than 100 yards from the house and barns. This stream runs alongside the road leading from the farm house, through the fields, to Lake Ellis, thus securing constantly good roads. There are two barns there. The house is a small unpainted building, good enough of the kind."

As we have noted, the land here had limited farming potential. One North Carolina agriculture map uses black to show counties with high agricultural output and various shades of gray to show counties with lesser yields. On that map eastern Craven County is white. Still there were a few places where soil conditions were right and where crops could be grown successfully.

In one example, Jack refers to Mr. Gorrell of Havelock, "an intelligent farmer" who owned 500 acres adjacent to Mr. Bryan and said he had been farming for 35 to 40 years, or since the end of the Civil War. The details about farmer Gorrell help in visualizing what life was like here at the turn of the last century.

"Mr. Gorrell, whose residence is near Havelock station, informs us that he sent by rail from

Havelock station 800 bushels of Irish potatoes from the 25th of May to the 25th of June. For 300 bushels, they received $4.00 per bushel. And for the balance $2.50. Their markets were New York and Philadelphia. The freight was 55 cents per bushel."

One place where a farm existed for many years is the site now occupied by the Wolfcreek subdivision. While we have no record at hand to suggest that this was Gorrell's farm, the Jack's location description is not inconsistent with it. The Gray Road area, Greenfield Heights, and Ketner Heights, among others, also had active farmland.

Mr. Gorrell states further: "We planted potatoes, corn, cotton, turnips, beets, peas, beans, onions, cabbages and peanuts on the sandy land under laid by clay which occurs at Havelock station, extending back toward the pocosin." Pocosin, from an Indian word meaning "rumbling earth" or shaky ground, refers to the water-saturated swampy land found here in abundance.

Jack gives dates when each crop is shipped by rail. "The railway company has run from one to three trains daily, carrying from 3,000 to 4,000 bushels on each train. The Steamer Neuse has made three trips per week from New Bern to Norfolk carrying 4,000 to 4,500 bushels. He estimated in the same paper that 350,000 bushels [of vegetables] had been carried from New Bern by railway and steamer."

Mr. Gorrell "gets this season $10 per ton for crab grass at the station at Havelock, and is unable to fill his orders. This grass grows naturally on the pocosin and this year he had about 40 acres in it which he told me yielded between 60 and 75 tons."

From the 1880s-1930s, Havelock's woods and water attracted sportsmen from across the nation. The rustic wilderness appealed to city dwellers in particular. Most came by rail. The prospectus refers to one of the people who vacationed here from across the East Coast: "A doctor from Philadelphia, who had a shanty on one of the lakeshores, where he had been spending several winters for his health, showed me two Black Bass...."

It is clear from the Bryan prospectus that the railroad continued to be a main piston of Havelock's economic engine. Whether it was people or produce, in 1899 riding the rails was the way to go.

Bryan's land was by and large the same tract owned by Richard Dobbs Spaight in colonial times. It had passed through other hands on the way to Bryan, of course, and Bryan's ownership eventually transferred as well. Over the years 8,800 acres were sold for the creation of Camp Bryan, the hunting and vacation hideaway down Lake Road. Much of the rest of the land was ultimately sold to the federal government as the core of the Croatan National Forest.

The prospectus offers one more delight: the earliest photograph we have of a Havelock railroad depot. This photo shows what would be the second depot building we know of; the first being the Union blockhouse beside Slocum Creek. The depot is a freight station that looks much like the current Havelock depot, but is on the opposite side of the tracks. A check of the underbrush at the site reveals the foundation of the building.

In addition to the Bryan prospectus we have another excellent source of local economic information from that period.

Branson's North Carolina Business Directory was published annually and contained the type of information you might find today in a chamber of commerce membership guide. *Branson's* staff went from town to town making lists of who was who and selling some advertisements along the way.

Havelock railroad depot, 1899

John B. Green, III Collection

The 1896 guide lists our local movers and shakers. Here we can glean the names of a couple of dozen prominent Havelock families.

A total of four general stores were operating at Havelock in 1896. The store's proprietors were:

John DePorte

M. N. Fisher

J. L. Garrell (probably "Mr. Gorrell" above)

Edward M. Piver.

The following men were the magistrates of Township Six:

J. H. Barnes

Dock Cooper

A. Jackson Chestnutt
    (husband of Laura V. Chestnutt)

James H. Hunter

E. H. Hess

John D. Pittman

Benj. E. Williams

Edward D. Russell (at Havelock)

Branson's also noted farmers. Havelock farmers in 1896 were:

T. W. Brame

J. A. Bryan (surely Maj. James A. Bryan)

John DePorte

James H. Hunter

W. H. Mallison

Henry Marshall

W. H. Pittman

J. D. Pittman

Mrs. Emeline Rone

A. J. Rone

Edward D. Russell

J. L. Stevenson

Mrs. Mary L. Taylor

G. T. Tippett

Vine Allen Tolson

J. P. Voliver

Benjamin E. Williams

No other professions or individuals were listed. The directory shows that at the end of the nineteenth century there were no hotels or boarding houses, no "manufactories," no doctors, lawyers or dentists, and very few families in Havelock, Craven County, North Carolina.

12
Riding the "Shoofly Express"

*U*ntil the coming of the Cherry Point Marine Corps Air Station in 1941, the railroad remained the centerpiece of local commerce and a blessed mainstay of local life. The train was depended upon to move people, products and letters from afar.

According to newspaper interviews with the Russell and Wynne families, for many years mail came on the evening train. The Havelock post office was always near the train station and at one time there was a tiny shed-like building with a crude, hand-carved PO HAVELOCK sign on it next to the freight depot on Lake Road. For many years, beginning on July 23, 1923, Walter James Wynne, Sr. was postmaster there.

Some years ago I visited the National Archives in Washington, D.C. Part of the research resulted in finding the names of all of the postmasters who served the numerous post offices here since the 1800s. Three men served as postmaster at Havelock in 1881: William Leauhouts, John Dinker and Edward D. Russell. Russell was in charge of the mail from then until 1898, except for a brief period in 1887 when C.H. Hunter stepped in. John I. Russell assumed command of the mail sacks in June 1898, followed by Sallie E. Russell in July, 1914. She was postmistress for nine years until Wynne took over.

Wynne was photographed outside his post office in 1942. He was a tall, thin man wearing a white shirt, hat and eyeglasses, with his ever-present cigar in hand. A black 1939 Plymouth sedan is parked nearby. Assisted daily by his wife, Maude, Wynne received sacks of mail from the train for a number of post offices including Harlowe, North Harlowe, Becton, Bachelor and Cherry Point. Folks responsible for those post offices would travel to Havelock to fetch their mail. The Havelock post office, measuring maybe 12 by 15 feet, was divided into two rooms. There were combination boxes inside, but most folks got their mail handed to them across the counter.

The Wynne family lived on Gray Road. Two of the sons, W.J., Jr. and Henry Clay, later played key roles in governmental and business growth here. W.J. served for 22 years as a Craven County commissioner and 43 years as a director of the Carteret-Craven EMC, the rural power co-operative. Clay became one of the founding commissioners of the town of Havelock. For many years, the pair also owned and operated one of the early service stations, Wynne Brothers Texaco on Main Street.

W. J. Wynne, Sr. served as postmaster until Havelock postal duties were transferred to New Bern in February, 1945. A small post office branch continued operation in the Commercial Shopping Center and was later replaced by a larger facility at the end of the same building. On January 1, 1957, Havelock gained its own postmaster again with the appointment of Mrs. Ruth Smith.

Like the mail, the rest of local life centered on the railroad crossroads as well. In 1886, some Havelock men cut timber and used oxen to drag it through the forest to a Newport sawmill. They hauled their fresh-cut lumber back to town and began the construction of the Havelock Methodist

Two-story general store and passenger railroad depot, Havelock, c. 1916

Edward Ellis Collection

Church on what is now Miller Boulevard. Soon a two-story general store, with the proprietors living upstairs, was built near where Trader's Store is today. Along with the rail depot, these buildings formed the social and commercial nexus of the community.

That old two-story store, of which we know little except what can be gleaned from a single photograph, existed until about 1916. It may be the one mentioned in *Branson's Business Directory* of 1890 as being operated at Havelock by C. H. Hunter.

It was owned for a time by E. A. and Martha L. Armstrong, but was sold to James A. Bryan on February 1, 1902, for $150. It had stables out back. A public "kitchen," an early version of a restaurant, was attached to the store. At one time it was known as "the Russell kitchen."

As we have noted, several other general stores were in business. Trader's Store followed in the early 1920s, having been rolled across the road on logs to its present location. It served the community into the 1970s.

For nearly 100 years, these country stores were the preferred gathering spots for all who lived nearby. Much of the stores' business revolved around the trains.

According to Mrs. Hugh Trader, interviewed by the New Bern *Sun-Journal* in 1976, there was a brisk business at Trader's Store on the days when all of Harlowe appeared to catch the train to New Bern. The trips by train took considerably longer than you might expect because the Mullet Line stopped at every crossroads and village.

"My children and I used to ride the train to Morehead City to visit relatives," Mrs. Trader said. "It wouldn't have taken so long to get there if the train hadn't stopped at every pea-patch: Newport, Wildwood, Mansfield...."

William "Bill" Jackson, in an undated interview in the late 1980s said, "When I was young...the only way out of Havelock was by train which went twice a day to Morehead City, New Bern and beyond on the Mullet Line which carried tobacco to New Bern [to big tobacco warehouses there] and wood which went to Kinston."

By 1941, when Cherry Point was being completed and staffed, the steam-powered train here was referred to as the "Shoofly Express." This has some of the connotations of the "Old Mullet Line" name, as all that fish attracted quite a few flying pests.

Writing in the *Windsock* in 1982, columnist Jack Murphy noted that "more than 20,000 military personnel, mainly Marines, were stationed at Cherry Point during the four years of World War II. Many of them came and went by rail and arrived at the Havelock train depot."

For many of them, their first stop was Trader's Store. The little store's financial status soared after 1940. In addition, millions of tons of material, supplies and equipment, were hauled by rail for construction of the base which was built at an initial cost just short of $100 million.

Later, Murphy wrote, "The mail trains and 'Shoofly Express' of the Atlantic and East Carolina Railroad became 'liberty' transportation to such places as the Pavilion at [Atlantic Beach] where airmen from Cherry Point and its outlaying fields will join with comrades in arms from Camp Lejuene to jitterbug to songs played by name bands and tell each other sea stories of adventurous battles as yet fought only in their imaginations... Soon these same railroad tracks would ring with the sound of troop trains carrying those new Marines on the first leg of a journey into real battles on the other side of the world..."

In fact, the railroad is a major reason MCAS Cherry Point was built here. The original plan was to build the base at Wilkerson Point, now known as Minnesott, in Pamlico County. At the last minute, with the inestimably significant involvement of Congressman Graham A. Barden, the plan was changed to the south side of the Neuse.

Lem S. Blades III, a descendent of the owners of the Blades Lumber Company, and for many years a local telephone executive and civic leader, stated in an August 26, 1987, letter:

"The critical factor was the need for a railroad. [Not only to supply the base, and reach the Port of Morehead, but also to connect it to Camp Lejeune]. Of course a bridge could have been built across the river to serve the northeast side [of the Neuse], but a bridge is militarily very vulnerable. [Not to mention expensive and vulnerable to storms]. To put a siding on land would have been very expensive, having to construct and acquire the right of way from Bridgeton to the site around Arapahoe."

Another factor was the happy coincidence of an enterprising businessman who brought the railroad out of receivership and renovated it just in time for the coming of Cherry Point. When Norfolk Southern defaulted on its lease during the Great Depression, the line was taken over by the State of North Carolina. Short of cash themselves, the state allowed the railroad to deteriorate to the point that it became dangerous. The line consisted of 11 worn-out locomotives running on badly rotted cross-ties and dilapidated trestles, every one of which needed repairs. A single train per day made the precarious roundtrip from Beaufort to Goldsboro.

In 1938, the governor tried to get the Southern Railway Company to take over the line.

Southern said the railroad was in such bad shape they would only take it if it came free of charge and if the state would pay any operating losses they incurred. The governor declined the offer.

Salvation came in 1939 in the form of railroad entrepreneur H.P. Edwards of Sanford. Edwards organized an operating company, raised funds, completed repairs, and started a locomotive program that saw the Old Mullet Line become one of the first railroads in the country to be all-diesel. This added the necessary encouragement the military needed to put the base on the south side of the Neuse. Shortly thereafter, tracks were built to Camp Lejuene. In 1957, after years of successful operation, Edwards sold the company at a tidy profit to, guess who, Southern Railway.

Blades shared the true story of a "great train robbery" here: "The first private railroad in Craven County was built by Blades Lumber Company from Havelock to Blades [near Harlowe]. It was a log hauling railroad [taking logs from the timberlands to the sawmills at Havelock where the lumber was sent out on the Mullet Line.] The engine was built on an old Cadillac auto chassis.

"The greatest train robbery of the day was a $200,000 plus robbery about 1910 near the Havelock express station. The payroll was for employees of Williams, James, and Charles Blades. The robbers were caught before sundown."

Peter Sandbeck, a historian with the North Carolina Division of Archives and History, wrote an interesting description of old Havelock in an article dated 1980.

"Old Havelock, located on the high ground between the east and west prong of Slocum Creek, has been encroached upon and nearly destroyed by modern suburban and strip development catering to the military population drawn to the area by the

Cherry Point Marine Corps Air Station," Sandbeck wrote.

The historian said "the area remained unnamed until 1857 when the Goldsboro to Morehead City line of the Atlantic and North Carolina Railroad reached this point" stating that at that time, "the crossing formed by the Beaufort Road and the railroad tracks was named Havelock..."

"The subsequent construction of a railroad freight and passenger depot stimulated development with a post office established by 1884, according to *Branson's North Carolina Business Directory* of the same year," Sandbeck noted.

Today, we have a photograph of a third Havelock railroad depot, this one from around 1916. It is the classic passenger design with an overhanging porch and "froo-frah" ornamentation along the roofline. The depot, located between the tracks and Lake Road, is larger than the current station, fancier by far, and appears to have telegraph wires into the building.

In 1976, referring to a time before 1940, Mrs. Hugh Trader said, "In those days the train station was located across the railroad tracks from its present site. And the overseers, Mr. and Mrs. Walter Walton, lived inside. The original train depot has since been destroyed and replaced by the gray [one] at the intersection of Nine Mile [Road] and Miller [Boulevard]."

Robert Dudley Fisher is the owner of Fisher Oil Company and life-long resident of Riverdale. On July 26, 2004, he told me that the current railroad freight depot at Havelock was moved there from Riverdale at the beginning of construction of Cherry Point.

The North Carolina Division of Archives and History describes our current railroad depot this way: "A one-story frame gable-front freight depot, built ca. 1940 on the site of the nineteenth century passenger and freight station. Exposed rafter ends, plain weatherboarding. Infrequently used."

In 1954, after military service, Fisher was offered a job working at the Havelock depot, by H.P. Edwards, the president and rescuer of the A&EC railway. "I thought that was the way to go. My father and grandfather had worked for the railroad, so I thought I would, too." He declined when he learned that the pay was $35 per month.

His father, Earnest Eric Fisher, (born 1900, died 1944) was freight agent at New Bern and then freight agent at Havelock after the beginning of WWII. One of the few photographs he has of his father shows him sitting on the steps of the freight depot when it was at Riverdale. His grandfather, Abram Dudley Fisher, was freight agent at Riverdale. Fisher said Riverdale was a "thriving little community" for a while with a sawmill, two brick kilns and a café.

Another memory of those times came from Thelma Dudley who grew up at Riverdale. Later in life a long-term resident of Clubfoot Creek, Mrs. Dudley remembered the busy days of Riverdale in a 1984 interview. "That was when the Roper Lumber Company was there," she said. "They were cutting timber and shipping it everywhere. Riverdale was booming then."

It was during the Roper timber boom that much of what would become the Croatan National Forest was clear-cut. Several of the more recent families of Havelock, like the Traders, arrived then, drawn here by employment in the lumber woods.

It took almost 30 years to cut down the forest. Much of the timber moved out via the railroad.

"By 1926 the timber boom was over," Mrs. Dudley said. "The timber company had removed all the timber and it moved on."

With it went much of the transient labor. The area saw another "out-migration" of residents as these jobs dried up. Except for moonshining, the next decade was pretty quiet here. The coming of Cherry Point and the Second World War changed all that. During the war a second passenger train was added daily because of all the servicemen coming and going.

Fisher said: "I rode that train many a time from Riverdale to New Bern. My daddy had a pass, you know, so I got to ride free. After a while the train got to where it didn't stop in Riverdale any more, but you could stand out there and wave a handkerchief or something and when he saw you he would 'toot-toot' to let you know he saw you, and then he'd stop." The train would always stop anywhere along its run if you flagged it down, he said.

The freight depot stood on the tracks at Riverdale directly behind the current location of Fisher Oil Company. Fisher's family home is nearby. Fisher does not recall how the depot was moved to Havelock, but believes it may have been moved there on the train.

Railroad passenger service existed for 92 years, but automobiles finally eliminated the customer base. The last passenger train ran on March 31, 1950. On the last run of the train all the customary stops were made including Havelock.

13

A Spaniard Spends the Night

We are getting too close to the present. Let's go back in time.

Have you heard the one about the traveling Spaniard and the innkeeper's daughter? In this recounting of a visit by a foreign observer to colonial America, Francisco de Miranda kisses and tells. His journal paints a descriptive picture of the region from New Bern to Beaufort at the end of the American Revolution.

Alexis de Tocqueville's 1830s classic *Democracy in America* is fairly well known to students of history. The book is a travelogue as well as social commentary by the young Frenchman who visited the United States to see for himself what had been created by our Founding Fathers.

Less well-known, but no less fascinating, is a similar book, *The New Democracy in America,* subtitled *Travels of Francisco de Miranda in the United States, 1783-84.* For us, Miranda's visit has more importance than Tocqueville's because Miranda came to Craven County. During a respite from his journey over much of the East Coast by land and sea, he socialized with the locals here and spent a memorable night just outside of what would become Havelock.

On June 1, 1783, Miranda left Cuba, "the home of vice and corruption," he said, on a voyage to the young American nation. He sailed aboard the American sloop *Prudent* arriving at Ocracoke, a small island on the North Carolina coast, at the entrance to Pamlico Sound.

Crayon portrait of Fransisco de Miranda

William Bennett Bizzell Memorial Library, University of Oklahoma

Miranda said residents of Ocracoke were robust and fat, attributing this to their food "which is nothing more than fish, oysters" and some garden vegetables, small gardens being "the only agriculture of these people that I know."

He said the Ocracokers were particularly afraid of smallpox and would not allow Miranda and his fellow passengers to leave their ship until they had made "a thousand protests that such disease was not with us on board."

Following the visit at Ocracoke, the *Prudent* entered the Pamlico on June 9, crossing into the Neuse River by the next morning. The voyage took him past the entrances to Handcock's and Slocumb's Creek on his way to the state capital and small port of New Bern. Miranda wrote that the Neuse River "in particular is large, its navigation pleasant, and its shores here and there covered with thick, luxuriant forests and some dwellings with little agriculture in their vicinity."

The traveler took a room at a New Bern inn and immediately began to make the acquaintance of not only the local leaders, but also the international visitors in New Bern during the Revolution. He extolled the hospitality and good treatment he was afforded "even though their ideas are not very liberal and the social system is still in swaddling clothes."

Then Miranda, the world traveler, unleashed this amazing paragraph about the Craven County society:

"The married women maintain monastic seclusion and a submission to their husbands such as I have never seen; they dress with neatness and their entire lives are domestic. Once married, they separate themselves from all intimate friendships and devote themselves completely to the care of home and family. During the first year of marriage they play the role of lovers, the second of breeders, and thereafter of housekeepers. On the other hand, the unmarried women enjoy complete freedom and take walks alone whenever they want to, without their steps being observed."

Miranda, referred to by one historian "an international Don Juan," may have carefully observed some of those young women's steps. The

Spaniard was less impressed with Craven County males.

"The men," he said, "dress carelessly and grossly. All smoke tobacco in pipes and also chew it, with so much excess that some assured me they could not go to bed and reconcile sleep without a cud in the mouth."

During the visit he became acquainted with local leaders Abner Nash, who had served as governor of North Carolina during the Revolution, and Col. Richard Dobbs Spaight, then 25, who would be governor 10 years later.

Miranda put the population of New Bern at "500 families." The houses are "middling and small as a rule, but comfortable and clean; almost all are made of wood." He noted that the church and assembly hall were brick and that the finest building "which really deserves the attention of an educated traveler is the so-called Palace," referring, of course, to Tryon Palace, the former home of the colonial governor.

Before leaving New Bern, Miranda was involved in a day celebrating the end of the War of Independence from Great Britain. News traveled slowly in those days so different parts of the country heard of the end of the war days, weeks, or even months apart. The local announcement, on June 17, of the preliminary treaty with England resulted in a military parade, the sound of drums, shots from cannon, a barbecue of roast pig and the tapping of a barrel of rum. He noted that "the leading officials and citizens of the region ate and drank with the meanest and lowest kind of people, holding hands and drinking from the same cup."

It is highly likely that some of the residents of Slocumb's Creek were at this celebration. The people in the outlying countryside looked to New Bern as a source of supplies and commerce, and, since New Bern was the state capital, for political leadership as well. Many of them also did business here. Nearly everyone used the courts. Some of them, like William Handcock, were intimately involved in political affairs themselves.

Though Wilmington had been seized and occupied by British general Lord Cornwallis, New Bern, for the most part, was spared direct military involvement. However, it was briefly invaded in August 1781 by British soldiers and Tories who shot and killed a prominent Patriot leader, Dr. Alexander Gaston. For good measure, they burned some warehouses, ships, and homes. The prospect of peace was warmly embraced by those here who had pulled together to make the Revolution a success.

While Miranda speaks of people "of the region" being in attendance he does not specifically mention anyone from eastern Craven County, nor does he say what social group, leaders or low, they would have been identified with. He says there were "some drunks, some friendly fisticuffs, and one man injured." The festivities ended with a bonfire of old barrels.

Miranda visited a farmer named "Mr. Green" who lived 12 miles from New Bern, but fails to say in which direction. There was a Green family who lived in our area, but there were others in the county as well. Whether this reference is to Slocumb's Creek we do not know. In any event, Miranda describes the country houses as comfortable and clean, though somewhat small. He says the inhabitants are industrious and "because of the war and general scarcity of manufactured good, every citizen set up a loom in his country house and made cotton and woolen clothes to dress the entire family." He mentions cider and brandy made from apples, pears, and peaches.

Back in New Bern he complains of the bedbugs and the noise of frogs.

On July 12, 1783, Miranda said farewell to his new friends, crossed the Trent River on a ferry and headed east on the road to Beaufort. At two in the afternoon he arrived at Always Inn, 23 miles from New Bern.

Some years ago, when I first read the story about the Always Inn, I set a trip odometer and drove in a car from New Bern following as closely as possible where I believe the Beaufort Road was in colonial days. I followed the route of old U.S. 70, what we now call the "Cherry Point Road." When that ran out at Flanner's Beach, I followed new U. S. 70 to Havelock where I turned onto Greenfield Heights Boulevard, then Miller Boulevard, and proceeded past the main gate of Cherry Point out Highway 101. My odometer had collected 23 miles when I got to that part of 101 in the area of Hancock Creek, Cahooque Creek Road and Ferry Road. Somewhere close by, in the late 1700s, would have been a place for travelers to eat and rest, the Always Inn.

We know from land grants that a large family named Always or Allways lived here. In 1755 Francis Always, a weaver, claimed 400 acres of land on Shop Branch, a tributary of Handcock's Creek, not far from where my odometer said the inn should be. A land warrant for John Benners on the east side of Handcock Creek, dated 1787, says Benners' 100-acre tract adjoined the line of Henry Always. In 1793, Obodiah Always was involved in a transaction with a James Potter for land at the head of Slocumb's Creek in the vicinity of modern Havelock. So, we know the Always family was here and we have a feel for where the inn might have been.

The location is an approximation as it is impossible to follow the precise course of the Old

Beaufort Road today. Also, Miranda may have been inaccurate about the 23 miles. We have maps today that show different mileages for the same road. Nevertheless, the preponderance of evidence points to this place just east of Havelock. The vicinity of Cahooque Creek Road makes sense because it is about one day's journey from New Bern. It is also halfway between New Bern and Beaufort, a well-traveled route, and therefore a convenient respite for the weary travelers of the day.

Now back to the story

Miranda described the road "as quite good, as they generally are in this area." He said, however, that recent rainstorms had resulted in all the low wooden bridges being destroyed by rising water. The wooden bridges he would have crossed on that trip are at the two prongs of Slocumb's Creek at Havelock where concrete bridges are today and possibly at Handcock's Creek as well.

With the bridges out, he continued the "tiring" trip, he says, "without horse and sulky." A sulky is a light two-wheeled, one-horse vehicle for one person. Since the vehicle could not cross the creeks, he apparently continued the journey on foot. It is doubtful he would simply have left the horse and sulky by the side of the road. He must have sold them or left them in the care of someone in "Havelock."

Matters improved significantly though when he reached Always Inn. Though tired, he was soon revived by "a moderate and clean meal and the company of Comfort and Constance, daughters of the innkeeper." The girls, Miranda guessed, were "15 to 18 years old, and very good looking."

At this point, Miranda goes to bragging.

"They soon made me forget the excursion," he said. "That evening there was supper and better conversation with the girls; after all had retired for the night, one had no embarrassment in coming at my request to continue the conversation in my bed."

Comfort and Constance were common names in that day and marriage bond records of Craven County later record the name of one of the young Always women. Six months after Miranda's visit, on January 29, 1784, Comfort married Roger James Jones, Jr. The Joneses were a large family of many descendents who had already lived nearby on the Neuse River for several generations. You will read about two of his ancestors in the next chapter. Many other Always women appear in the old county marriage records, but I have found no reference to Constance. Perhaps Miranda got the name wrong when writing later in his journal.

A history of the Loftin family was published in 1936. An entry there says Sarah Loftin, the daughter of Leonard Loftin, married Henry Always. Leonard Loftin later deeded property to Henry Always. And then the zinger: Henry and Sarah had two children, Comfort and Content. This would make Henry and Sarah Loftin Always the proprietors of Always Inn in the 1780s, but there is still no further reference to Content, whose name the Spaniard Miranda misunderstood.

At six o'clock the next morning, presumably before Mr. Always awoke, Miranda left for Beaufort, 21 miles away. On the journey he described crossing "a swamp which must have been more than a mile wide and had millions of mosquitoes." That "swamp," a low place filled in both directions by standing water and marsh grass, is still there and easily seen shortly before arriving in Beaufort via Highway 101.

He lodged for a few days in Beaufort which he described as having "no commerce" and whose residents he described as "poor." He noted that

Beaufort had 80 citizens and described their homes as "miserable."

Miranda soon boarded a schooner for the continuation of his East Coast tour. This time he headed for Charleston, much to the delight, no doubt, of South Carolina womanhood.

14

What Happened to the Local Indians?

I promised myself a long time ago that I would never watch another Indian movie because they all end the same way: badly. This chapter does not end any better. It has savagery, murder, and, in the end, well, genocide. There is no other word for it. What commends its retelling is that these events happened here.

Had you been in Craven County in the early 1700s you would have been scared. You would have smelled the smoke from the burning homes. You would have heard shots fired in anger and possibly screams and shouts. Very probably you would have known some of the victims of the massacres.

Standing on the banks of the Neuse River near the mouth of Slocum Creek, it is easy to see why the first white European settlers arriving around 1690 considered this place a paradise. Those first settlers, French Huguenots, came here seeking religious and political freedom.

Huguenots were Protestants who followed the teachings of John Calvin. The movement began in the 1500s and found followers in all classes of French society, despite severe harassment and steady persecution by the country's ruling monarchy.

The St. Bartholomew's Day Massacre in Paris on August 24, 1572, began two months of slaughter and the death of thousands of Huguenots. Finally, in 1598, King Henry IV put an end to the madness with the Edict of Nantes. The edict granted civil rights and some religious freedom to Huguenots in some parts of France, but not in Paris itself. Catholic pressure, however, led to a revocation of the edict by Louis XIV in 1672, the resumption of persecution, and the flight of many Huguenots to America.

Within a few years, a group of these religious and political refugees settled here along the Neuse River. In this place, a paradise of natural bounty, they found the freedom they so desperately sought. They also found something else: the primitive-appearing natives they called the Indians.

Before the coming of the settlers, a large population of indigenous tribal people roamed freely here. Far from primitive, they built villages and towns, controlled their own territories, engaged in commerce, practiced religion, and occasionally fought one another. But with their unique customs, dress, and language, they were judged by the Europeans to be backward and savage.

Today there is a half-moon shaped point of land on the Neuse River that nearly caps the mouth of Slocum Creek. On that point of land, easily seen from the Cherry Point Officers Club, we now know an Indian village existed. Archaeologists working there in recent decades have found pottery and other artifacts proving the site was occupied for at least 400 years. Modern maps show that the locale was the ideal place for a settlement of Neusiok Indians. Surrounded on three sides by water, the point was easier to defend than nearby woodlands. Elevations of up to 15 feet provided protection against the rising water of storms. And, with a diet consisting largely of fish, crabs and clams, breakfast was literally at the backdoor.

The Neusiok, for whom, as you may have guessed, the Neuse River was named, numbered about 1,000 when the settlers began to arrive. The Indians had a thriving culture as fishermen, hunters and farmers, and a 20-mile long road to the Newport River and nearby Bogue Sound called the Neusiok Trail. The trail connected them to their cousins, the Coree tribe, on the sound. It still exists to this day preserved within the Croatan National Forest.

You know the story: The Indians were at first tolerant of the immigrants. There was trade, some socializing, some friendship, but things turned nasty as more and more settlers arrived.

One year after the founding of New Bern by Swiss and German settlers in 1710, a full-scale war broke out. The Neusiok and the Coree were "tributary tribes" of the much larger Tuscarora confederation. The confederation also included the Woccon, Bay, Chowan, Bear River, Pamlico, Wachapunga, and others and was led by a mighty chieftain, King Hancock.

Among the first events of the coming war was the kidnapping of New Bern's Swiss founder. New Bern, named for Berne, Switzerland, was laid out in neat rectangular plots by Baron Christopher de Graffenried and the English explorer and surveyor John Lawson. Graffenried and Lawson, accompanied by two slaves, set out by canoe in the fall of 1711 to explore the river north of New Bern. A few miles up the Neuse, the group was captured and taken prisoner by Indians who simply walked out into the shallow water and surrounded them.

Details from historical accounts vary and sometimes contradict one another. This version provides the gist of the story.

The natives had a large, heavily-fortified town above New Bern in what is now Greene County. The captives were taken to King Hancock and were held and interrogated for several days before Lawson was executed in a particularly gruesome manner. The way the story has come down is that slivers of wood were stuck into Lawson one at the time until his entire body was covered with these painful, wooden projections. Then, in the presence of Graffenried, the slivers were set on fire burning Lawson to death.

The kidnapping of Lawson and Graffenreid.

North Carolina Collection, The University of North Carolina at Chapel Hill

The execution of Lawson is another of the unexplainable curiosities of history, as no one had been more sympathetic to, or more knowledgeable of, the Indians than Lawson. One of the earliest explorers here, Lawson lived "with a Young Indian Fellow and a Bull-Dog" on the creek named for him at New Bern. He called the Indians "fine specimens of humanity."

The Indians killed him anyway and kept the two slaves so they could sell them.

After the killing, Graffenried was held for six weeks. Here the versions differ again saying that he made peace, offered ransom for himself, or was released after being told by King Hancock that he and his kind should go back to where they had come from. Before Graffenried could return to New Bern, however, the Indians attacked.

Most of the settlers died in a single day of terror, September 22, 1711, when some 500 Indian warriors silently infiltrated both the scattered farms and more densely populated settlements of the entire region and struck without warning. About 150 men, women, and children were killed in two hours after the coordinated dawn attack. Torture was common. Stakes were driven through the bodies of the women. Eighty of the dead were said to be young children. Others were kidnapped and made captives, particularly women and children. The killing continued for several days. Homes and barns were ransacked and burned. Livestock was killed. Property was plundered. Many were left wounded.

About half of the dead were members of the New Bern colony. New Bern was temporarily abandoned in favor of the fortified plantation of Capt. William Brice, across the Trent River along the creek that still bears his name.

During the Tuscarora War of the next four years nearly a third of the white settlers and virtually all the Indians were killed. Farming was disrupted. Times were hard. After Virginia refused to help and nearby North Carolina Quakers refused to fight, colonial forces from South Carolina marched to the local settlers' defense. The leader of the expeditionary force was Col. John Barnwell, an Irishman. He established his base in northern Craven County and the hamlet there is still called Fort Barnwell today. Oddly enough, his force of some 550 men consisted mostly of South Carolina Indians. One authority, Steve Thompson, called these Pee Dee Indians "ancient enemies of the Tuscarora."

Before Barnwell's arrival in January of 1712, the settlers led several retaliatory attacks. After the larger force arrived, the struggle became a fight to the death between the two sides. Indian villages were besieged, attacked and burned. There were several major engagements involving hundreds of fighters. In one battle in 1713, state records say 950 Indians were killed or taken prisoner. But, mostly, day to day, both sides hunted one another. Virtually any encounter between whites and Indians turned to bloodshed.

At Havelock, Evan Jones and his brother, Roger, sons of Welsh Quaker pilgrims, were chased through the woods by Indians. The pair was attacked while working at their turpentine distillery in timber near Evan's home. The Jones farm was located on property now occupied by the Cherry Point Officers Club. That morning in 1712, Evan Jones managed to escape, but Roger was killed by the small band of marauders.

Graffenried, who had been the undisputed leader of the New Bern colony, never regained his stature after being accused, many think unfairly, of a failure of leadership resulting in the massacre. Within a year, he sold his property to Thomas Pollock and returned to Europe for good. The disaster would haunt him for the rest of his days.

If the settlers had a hard time, the Indians faired even worse. In 1715, the colonial government ordered the "Entire Destruction of ye said nation of

Indians as if there had never been a peace made with them." By year's end the hostilities were over. The local Neusiok tribe was gone, either killed outright or the victim of new illnesses brought by the settlers. A few Neusiok escaped and migrated north to join related tribes in New York.

A paltry number of Indians remained. Some had sided with the settlers against the main bands they considered rivals. This was especially true of some Corees who had traditionally traversed the Neusiok trail to fish on the Neuse River at Cherry Point. The few survivors would have lived in peace, keeping mostly to themselves, but eventually interbreeding with whites and, later, with black freedmen until their pure blood disappeared.

Archeologists tell us that the indigenous people had been here for 12,000 years or more. But two short decades after the arrival of the first white European settlers, and 61 years before the signing of the Declaration of Independence, those native Americans had ceased to exist in coastal Carolina.

15
Our Hero and Namesake

*M*y historical research began with the quest for an explanation of how our little whistle-stop in the piney woods came to be named Havelock. I was 12 or 13 when I went for answers to the tiny Havelock library branch on Miller Boulevard. Tiny, indeed, as the library shared its small square building with the driver's license and sheriff's offices.

At the time there was a single paragraph of Havelock history in the slender telephone book. That paragraph made the claim that our community had been named for Sir Henry Havelock, a British war hero. I came to the library that day to review what information might be on hand about this man and to understand why his name had been chosen for our town.

Much to my chagrin, the duty librarian informed me that there was no information on Sir Henry Havelock. There was not a single book, pamphlet, brochure, or article. Nothing. Not to be denied, I pulled the appropriate Encyclopedia Britannica from the shelf and found a succinct entry describing his exploits. There was no mention of Havelock, N.C., of course, or any explanation of why his name was selected for this place. There was something curious in the encyclopedia entry, though. It appeared he had never been here or anywhere near here. In fact, Henry Havelock had never been to the United States of America. Born in England, he had spent the bulk of his life in India.

India! How could this be?

I was hooked. I had to know.

Today, I have reams of information on the man. Dozens of his many portraits are in my files. I have corresponded with and/or visited almost all the places called Havelock in the world. What may very well be the largest collection of books on Maj. Gen. Sir Henry Havelock this side of the British Museum in London graces my shelves. There are 56 volumes in all and some are more than 140 years old. Included are two rare volumes penned by the general himself. There are Henry Havelock artifacts, including post cards, postage stamps, trading cards, prints, photographs, a musical score, and a British army medal for temperance called "the Havelock." In other words, Henry Havelock has been a wonderful hobby. I have come to know him well. He is one of my heroes. In all that I have learned of him, he has never let me down.

First and foremost, Henry Havelock was a devout Christian. Exceptionally fervent in his belief, exceedingly rigid in his manner, he was considered a "crank" by some who served with him in colonial India. Second, he was a consummate military man. In the end, he was an excellent leader and as good a general as ever took men into battle. Finally, he was a remarkable and devoted family man.

Besides his wife and children, his two lifelong passions were the odd combination of Bible study and the mastery of military tactics. He conducted himself without concern for the judgment of others focusing always on what he thought was proper and important. In the end, matters came out right.

Maj. Gen. Sir Henry Havelock

Edward Ellis Collection

Havelock was born on April 5, 1795, at Ford Hall, the family's estate at Bishop-Wearmoth, England. He was the second son of a prosperous shipbuilder, William Havelock (1757-1837).

Here is another of those odd curiosities of history. Being a shipbuilder, there is some degree of probability that William Havelock received and used naval stores produced at and shipped from a place that would someday bear his son's name. You will recall that the Slocum's Creek area of Craven County accounted for nearly one-quarter of the world's production of these products used to build ships. Isn't it fun to imagine barrels in England on the Havelock shipyard docks labeled "Product of Slocum's Creek?"

Once again, I digress.

Henry's mother, Jane, was responsible for the strong moral upbringing referred to in almost all accounts of his life. He was only 16 when he lost her guidance. She died in 1811.

Havelock's relationship with his father was rocky at best. The loss of his mother and his father's coming professional ruin only compounded matters. Due to unsuccessful speculation, William suffered financial troubles and lost much of his fortune in 1812. Henry and his father disagreed about the son's career. William wanted him to become a lawyer. That was the last thing on Henry's mind. In 1814, after a blow-up with his father, Henry left school. With the help of his older brother, also named William, he received a commission as a lieutenant in the British army. William had distinguished himself in several battles including Waterloo and got Henry a posting with the 95th Regiment on July 30, 1815.

A few years later the young lieutenant was ordered to India. The India of Henry Havelock's time, with its battles between the occupying British troops and the native population, was much like the American Wild West. British forces also engaged in nearly constant battle with Afghans and Sikhs. A young officer looking for experience could not have been in a better place.

During the long sea voyage to India, Havelock underwent the religious conversion that would color the remainder of his days. One biographer says Havelock embraced Christian principles following a violent storm at sea that nearly cost him his life. Another has it that during the long voyage around Africa, a brother officer, Lt. James Gardner, was the instrument of his conversion. In any event, when Havelock arrived in Calcutta in May 1823, he was a changed man.

More changes were on the way. We are told that Havelock conducted himself well in battle. He took part in campaign after campaign in the hot, dusty land. In 1824, he took a fifty percent cut in pay to join the 13th Light Infantry in the first Anglo-Burmese War. The fighting lasted two years.

In 1829, Havelock married Hannah Shepard Marshman, the daughter of a famous minister and became a Baptist.

He gained rank slowly. In 1838, after more than 20 years of service he was only a captain. That year he took part in the First Afghan War. Some writers have speculated that Havelock was often passed over for advancement because of his ardent Christian faith and his strong stand against alcohol. At one point, five other officers were promoted over him. Still, he was recognized for his skill on the battlefield. He was made a "Companion of the Bath," an honor close to knighthood. He also began drawing to him a group of like-thinking individuals whose temperance made them reliable soldiers.

One night there was an attack on a British barracks by marauding natives. The commander was told that the guard detail was drunk and unable to respond. The commander roared, "Call out Havelock's Saints. His men are never drunk and he is always ready." That night, Havelock and his troops did what needed to be done. The nickname "saints" for Havelock and his men had first been used in ridicule, but came to be spoken with a grudging respect. They were known for their faith, sobriety and skill in battle.

The governor-general of India, Sir Henry Hardinge, would later say that Havelock "was every inch a Christian, every inch a soldier."

Havelock and his troops would rise before reveille to hold religious services. Sometimes they would go into the solemn darkness of a nearby Buddhist temple and there, under the very gaze of the statue of Buddha, they would lift their voices in worship of their Christian savior.

The skill and faith of Havelock's Saints would be sorely tested in the whirlwind of history that was to unfold in 1857; a tumult that would rival any challenge ever faced by an army, and a series of events that would propel Henry Havelock to the very pinnacle of world fame.

By 1849, Havelock had been in India for 26 years. During that time, for lack of money to buy rank and because he was considered a grouchy eccentric by some, he had been passed over for promotion 22 times. Still he had earned experience, medals and respect for his conduct on the battlefield. He had fought in many campaigns, had horses shot from beneath him and learned what it took to win in war. Slowly, recognition began to come. He was promoted to quartermaster-general of the Queen's troops in India, then to lieutenant colonel and brevet colonel. When the post of adjutant general opened in 1854, he was named to fill the position.

In November 1856, war was declared between England and Persia. Havelock, under Sir James Outram, was given a division to command and was ordered to the Persian Gulf. It was his last engagement before the Sepoy Mutiny, the bloody uprising that would make him famous.

16
The Sepoy Mutiny

*T*he Sepoy Mutiny of 1857 should never have happened. The immediate cause of the uprising was one of the most stupid public relations blunders in the history of mankind.

Here are the details:

The Sepoy were native troops who sided with the British occupying force in India. The British never numbered more than 100,000 inside a nation of millions. Paid and supplied by England, the Sepoy were used to keep the native population in line. These hired warriors were feared by the people at large. They could be ruthless and cruel in suppressing unrest.

The Sepoy were made up mostly of Hindus and Moslems. Hindus considered the cow to be sacred. The Moslems considered the pig to be unclean. In 1857, the British issued a new rifle, the cartridge of which was greased with pig and cow fat. Even more objectionable, the Sepoy had to bite off the end of the cartridge before loading it into the rifle. The native troops actually had to put the foul material into their mouths.

Their complaints fell on deaf British ears. When a group in Delhi threw down their weapons, they were threatened at gunpoint by British soldiers, and the fighting commenced. Within days, the word spread that native regiments at Delhi,

Ferozepore and Meerut had mutinied. With great loss of life, Delhi had fallen into their hands.

When the native population saw that the Sepoy had rebelled, they took it as a signal that the time had come for a revolution. All over India, British embassies, compounds and residences were besieged by angry mobs bent on killing the imperialists. All of the worst of human nature came forth, as it often does at times like these. Killing, rape, looting and arson were rampant and the British men, women and children were the objects of the wrath.

Havelock returned from his successful campaign in the Persian Gulf on May 19, 1857, and learned of the mutiny when he reached Bombay. He set out immediately to join a relief column marching on Delhi. The relief force was headed by Gen. George Anson, the commander-in-chief in India. The best up-country route was then in the hands of the mutineers so Havelock embarked on a ship called the *Erin*.

It was not a good trip. The *Erin* wrecked on the coast and he had to wait to be picked up by another vessel that was dispatched for him from Calcutta. Havelock reached Madras on June 13 and learned that Gen. Anson was dead. A local commander, Sir Patrick Grant, had replaced Anson. Havelock went with Grant and they arrived in Calcutta on June 17, five weeks after the start of the rebellion. With India's military leadership in disarray, Havelock stepped to the fore. He was promptly given command of the entire force at Allahabad. His son, also named Henry, was with him now and served as his aide-de-camp. Havelock's orders were ambitious. He was to put down all resistance in the area, to move swiftly to support Sir Hugh Wheeler at Cawnpore and Sir

Henry Lawrence at Lucknow, and, oh yes...to disperse and destroy all the Sepoy mutineers.

Within days Havelock's force was en route to Cawnpore, a central Indian city under siege by mutinous native troops. Havelock had heard on July 3 that many British soldiers and officials had been slaughtered there, but several hundred more European women, children and a few men were still alive and surrounded in the fortress-like embassy.

With his army of 1,000 soldiers, a few volunteer horsemen and six cannons, Havelock moved across India during the hottest season of the year. By forced march he headed for his goal 126 miles away, stopping time and again to engage and defeat rebel forces. As Havelock's victories mounted, word began to be carried to Europe and England of his successes. Back home people were astonished by the brutality of the uprising and were waiting daily for dispatches from India. Nearly every newspaper in Europe carried stories of the Indian mutiny. The stories made it to America as well. Havelock's name began to appear in print around the world.

On July 15, Havelock again received word that the hostages were holding out at Cawnpore; however a hideous drama was unfolding, even as he marched to the rescue. The local rebel leader's name was Nana Sahib. He has been painted as a ruthless and corrupt criminal. Among his many crimes, he was alleged to have killed a man so he could steal the victim's wife.

The Nana, leader of the Cawnpore mutineers, told the British citizens trapped in the embassy that he wished them no harm. He said he merely wanted them to leave the place. He sent word that he would supply boats for their get-away on the river. For the hostages, the offer was most tempting. The mothers had very little water and food for their children.

They were suffering from the heat and reeling from the shock of having seen husbands and friends killed. The thought of escape must have been irresistible. After much deliberation, they decided to go. Gathering what few possessions they could carry, the surviving men, women and children left the compound where they had been held for weeks. Moving carefully, they made their way down to the river.

Soon most had boarded the boats. The rest were standing in long rows on the stone steps at the river's edge waiting their turns. It was at that moment that Nana Sahib ordered the hidden guns uncovered and had his men open fire on the unarmed people.

They were slaughtered.

Amid screams and cries, five men were able to make it to the opposite river bank. All but one were hunted down and killed. That single survivor lived to tell the tale of Nana Sahib's treachery.

After the butchery, the rebel leader moved out with 5,000 men to confront Havelock and his force of less that 1,000. It would be one of the telling battles of the mutiny. The two armies met on July 16, 1857, a few miles outside of Cawnpore. Through what has been described as a "masterly flanking movement," Havelock used his forces to send Sahib's fighters into disarray. Members of Havelock's small force charged directly into cannons and right up the enemy's batteries and began capturing guns and turning them on the mutineers.

Fighting went on all day before the rebels were all killed or ran away. Nana Sahib fled the battlefield. He is said to have escaped to Nepal and was never captured or punished for his deeds. *The Illustrated London News* later wrote "the name of Nana Sahib will for the future stand conspicuous as that of the most ruthless and treacherous scoundrel who ever disgraced humanity."

Victorious against huge odds, Havelock and his men stopped for the night about two miles from the city. Havelock had now marched the 126 miles under a blazing Indian sun, fighting and winning four major engagements against superior numbers along the way. The next morning they entered Cawnpore.

What they found there is among the saddest scenes of human history. The bodies of the women and children were scattered along the river. Many of them had been dumped down a well possibly while still alive. The horror of the well would resonate in Great Britain becoming a long-remembered source of anguish and anger. One biographer cites Havelock's hold on his men as the reason few atrocities were committed against the captured mutineers: "The pitiful scene presented by the remains of their murdered fellow countrymen exasperated them to madness, but the firm hand of their commander held them in check."

The rigors of battle, the lack of a steady supply of food, and illness began to take its toll upon Havelock's small force. The decaying bodies did not help matters. Havelock moved his men outside the city so they could rest. He knew there was much to be done.

A force of 100 soldiers was ordered by the general to secure Cawnpore and deal with the dead. Soon Havelock and his remaining 800 fighters were marching again, this time to try and save another group of besieged English citizens at a town called Lucknow.

Back home in England, and in other parts of the world, readers waited anxiously for the next newspaper report of the fate of those in the Lucknow Residency. Trapped inside, surrounded and under attack, were British men, women and children many of whom would die as a result of the rebel onslaught. Having heard of the horrors of Cawnpore, the public had good reason to fear the worst at Lucknow. Havelock was their one hope.

At Bithoor, outnumbered five to one, Havelock defeated a rebel force of 4,000. Taking personal command in the field from horseback, he would win nearly a battle a day for the rest of the march.

Throughout his career, Havelock had been passed over for promotions and command. Now at the height of his achievement, while literally the whole world was watching his exploits in India, came word that Sir James Outram had been appointed to command the area where Havelock had skillfully assumed control. When Outram arrived with reinforcements on September 15 he found Havelock making preparations for a move on Lucknow. Outram then made a decision that one writer called "one of the most memorable acts of self-abnegation recorded in military history." Outram relinquished his rank and offered to accompany Havelock as a civilian volunteer.

When Havelock left Cawnpore on September 19, he was in command of 3,000 men. Under fire as they crossed the Ganges, Havelock's force would fight for the next 60 days almost without ceasing. He drove the enemy from Mungalwar, captured Bunnee, and attacked the Allumbugh, a fortified position within sight of Lucknow where the hostages were held.

The fight was an urban battle now. Nearly all of the enemy forces had concentrated at Lucknow for what was expected to be the major event of the conflict. The two sides fought fence to fence, bridge to bridge, building to building, in a fierce contest for possession of the city. Havelock's force fought its way in among the enemy finally reaching the residency where the British citizens were housed. There was unimaginable relief for the captive countrymen in the compound.

The British residency in Lucknow had been a spacious, elegant building inside a large walled compound. It served as both embassy offices and quarters for the British staff and their families. After being shelled for two months, the building resembled a huge block of Swiss cheese. The random and incessant bombardment had been a living hell for the people within.

Having fought its way to the center of the city Havelock's force now had enemy troops on all sides. From the residency stronghold, he and his men, along with the rescued British citizens, began to force the enemy from surrounding buildings and take more ground. It was not until another force, under the command of Sir Colin Campbell, arrived on November 16 that the Indians were brought under control. With the fall of Lucknow, for all intents and purposes, the Sepoy Mutiny was over.

Upon the arrival of Campbell, Havelock learned that his fame had spread around the world. The 62-year-old soldier was informed he had been promoted to major general. He had also been knighted by the Queen of England as he fought his way across the dusty landscape of India.

He was now Maj. Gen. Sir Henry Havelock.

17
How Havelock Got Its Name

*N*ews of the death of Maj. Gen. Havelock on November 24, 1857, shook Great Britain like a thunderbolt.

Stories of his exploits had been the only source of hope during the dark days of the Indian Mutiny in which thousands lost their lives. After years laboring in obscurity, he had become a national hero. His name was known around the world.

Gen. George Patton, an icon of World War II, was later to put forth the proposition that a warrior should die from the last bullet of the last battle. Havelock died very soon after his last battle was fought. Four days following the relief of Lucknow, he fell ill with dysentery. Dysentery, common in that place and time, is a painful inflammation of the large intestine resulting in fever and internal bleeding. The 62-year-old soldier had been fighting for months under the blazing tropical sun. His last portraits show a skinny, tired-looking man.

At his death he was surrounded by many of his friends. His son, who would one day also be a major general, was with him, too. He told them that he was happy and content. "See how a Christian dies," he said.

Four days after he was taken ill, barely a week after his final battle, Havelock was dead.

News of his passing did not reach England until January 7, 1858, and the nation plunged into mourning. Every newspaper in England carried word of his death as did most in Europe and many in America. The *New Bern Union* reported the death of Havelock in India.

The Sunday following the news of his death, a memorial service was held in his honor in every village, town and city in England. At Havelock's home church, Bloomsbury Baptist, an overflow crowd of 1,000 had to be turned away and the service repeated the following week.

Even Queen Victoria was said to have been distressed by Havelock's passing.

In America, flags were lowered to half-mast in New York and Philadelphia, the first time this honor had ever been shown for a British citizen. America, which had fought multi-year wars with England in 1776 and 1812, had not acknowledged the recent death of the Duke of Wellington by lowering flags. But flags were lowered for Havelock.

An honorary editorial appeared in the *New York Times*.

Public donations were gathered for the construction of a huge bronze statue of Havelock in London's Trafalgar Square where it is to this day. In Guild Hall, the equivalent in London of City Hall, a bust of the general was placed and paid for with tax money.

Havelock's wife, Hannah, received such a pension by order of Parliament that the family was left comfortable for several generations. Havelock's son, Henry, who served gallantly as his aide-de-camp, was knighted and made a baronet.

Havelock was buried in India.

An excerpt from a biography by Sir Leslie Stephens could serve as his eulogy: "Gifted with military ability of a high order, Havelock had been employed for the greater part of his career in subordinate positions, to which his want of means, and probably also a certain sternness of disposition, combined with an earnest, but somewhat narrow religious profession, had contributed to confine him. A soldier of the old Puritan type, his highest aim was to do his duty as service rendered to God rather than to his superiors, while the constant submission of himself to God's will enabled him to bear with cheerfulness his many disappointments and long waiting for that recognition of his power which he coveted, and made him resolute and devoted in the discharge of duties no matter how small. When the opportunity came, he proved himself to be a great military leader, and won the gratitude of his country."

Havelock's life could serve as an object lesson about the fragility of fame. For a brief moment in late 1857 and early 1858, he was among the most famous men alive. His military achievements were Olympian. His life was a shining example of selfless service to God, country, and family. His death only compounded his fame and brought a worldwide outpouring of both grief and adulation.

Now, except in a few small places, he is a forgotten man.

Why is he remembered here in the name of this city? To understand that, we must return to the entity that has had so much impact here, in so many ways: the railroad.

While Havelock toiled half a world away to save his besieged countrymen, a railroad was being built through the forests of eastern North Carolina. Many of the future stops had names. New Bern is an example. When the new rail line crossed some road or a waterway and created a new stopping point for the train, a name had to be chosen. Here,

Slocum's Creek would have been an obvious choice. The big name in the news, however, was Havelock.

Tales of Sir Henry's exploits were the talk of the year and captivated the imagination of the world. His story was covered in local newspapers, as was his death. The publication of his biography in England by his brother-in-law, John Clarke Marshman, was noted in a newspaper in New Bern.

Within months of his death, eight cities around the world were named for Havelock. Two are in New Zealand where there is a Havelock on one island and a North Havelock on another. One, now renamed, was in Swaziland in southern Africa. Two are in Canada; in Ontario and New Brunswick. Three are in the United States. There is a Havelock, Iowa, a Havelock, Nebraska, and, of course, Havelock, North Carolina.

There is an island in the Indian Ocean called Havelock Island. Around the world, there are streets, schools, churches and geographical features named for him that are too numerous to mention.

An item of headgear invented and popularized by the general and common among his troops also bears his name. A cap cover with a flap hanging over the back to protect the neck from the sun is called a "havelock." It was used by the troops in India and was later worn by the French Foreign Legion.

Havelock became a favorite inspirational symbol for Civil War soldiers. His name and likeness appeared on some common items purchased and carried by those soldiers. One is called a Union case. It was a little hinged book-like affair used to protect tintype portraits of loved ones. The Union cases were made from a primitive plastic called gutta-percha, which provided some water resistance. One of the most popular Union cases carried by soldiers in the war had a standing image of Sir Henry holding a sword and the name "Havelock" molded on both the front and back.

There is no known evidence that documents the selection process for the name of our rail stop. Perhaps a single railroad bureaucrat had the duty. Perhaps local people and railroad officials agreed on the name. When the local crossing was named Havelock Station, the next rail stop was named Lucknow Station after Sir Henry's most famous battle. That name did not stick. It was soon changed to Shepardsville. Today, we call it Newport.

Correspondence with people in the other Havelocks confirms they were named for Sir Henry. Mrs. Sharyn Cook of Havelock, Iowa, said she and her husband visited Havelock, N.C., once. She had her first taste of stuffed crab here. Patricia Downey of the Lincoln Public Library told us that Havelock, Nebraska, now overgrown by Lincoln, was indeed named for our man.

The only people who never responded were officials in Swaziland. That region has spent a lot of time changing the names in their country back to ones used before the British colonial period. Others have confirmed that Havelock, Swaziland, was named for the general. A postage stamp commemorates the site of the world's largest asbestos mine there. It is, as you would expect, the Havelock Mine.

With 56 books to select from, the gentle reader will understand that many details have been culled from this brief report. There is much more that could be said, but the important things are covered. Henry Havelock was a good father, a loving and devoted husband, a leader of men, a man of principle and superior professional skill. When called upon, he was ready to do his duty and accomplished, in a profoundly heroic manner, the tasks fortune laid before him.

Henry Havelock provided inspiration for those around him. The wide-spread story of his life gave inspiration for our predecessors. The retelling of the story of his strong character, bravery under fire and military genius offers us inspiration today. There are names within the pantheon of history that may bring equal credit upon a community, but there are few names, when all is said and done, that should be held in higher esteem than that of Havelock.

18
Send in the Marines

*C*herry Point is gone.

You may be surprised to hear that, but it is definitely true. It is gone, washed away. The real Cherry Point is not where the Marine base is situated, but on the point of land east of there, to the east of Hancock Creek, at the end of Ferry Road.

A look at any good map, like a U.S. Coast and Geodetic Survey chart, will still show Cherry Point at that location. The point itself, as it existed 100 years ago, has been eroded away by the ever-pounding forces of the Neuse River. Erosion increased with the digging of the modern channel for the state ferry. Now the "point" is gone along with the cherry orchard that once grew there. What is there on the remnant of the real Cherry Point, on either side of the state ferry, is a residential subdivision.

The name is preserved on the west side of Hancock Creek and the Marine base because of the "landing." The easy place for boats to load and unload from colonial times onward, was on the western edge of the mouth of Hancock Creek and was known as Cherry Point Landing. This site is "on base" where the Hancock Yacht Club and the Navy docks are today.

Using transient and local labor, a lumber company, either Blades or Roper, once timbered a huge tract of land where the base was later built. Much of the land was owned in the 1930s by the N.C. Pulp Company. Tradition says one of the timber companies established a small post office that used as its location the name "Cherry Point." So, the name sort of migrated westward even though the real, original Cherry Point is somewhat east of there.

In any event, National Archive records show a post office was opened on November 12, 1890. The first Cherry Point postmaster was David W. Morton, Jr. In 1893, Austin N. Weaver took over to be relieved by Molly E. Morton the next year. In those days, the postmaster's home usually served as the post office. In 1901, B.D. Borden assumed the task and served until Annie Russell became postmistress in July 1907. Mrs. Russell served until the Cherry Point post office duties were transferred to Havelock effective January 1, 1932.

The landing is where the Russell family, their extended family and neighbors, about 30 people altogether, lived in the early 1900s. These were the relatives and friends of the people who lived in Havelock, some seven miles away by buggy, mule cart, on foot, and in more recent times, by primitive automobile.

Here at Cherry Point landing among others lived "Captain" George Allen Russell. Born in 1876, he was a farmer and Neuse River buoy tender, married to Annie Breslin Russell, who emigrated from Brackey Ardora, County Donegal, Ireland, in 1891.

Darrow and Madge Wetherington kept a small grocery and general store there. Nearby were several other families, a community cemetery, a school, and hunting and fishing camps, like the Smithfield Lodge and the Kinston Camp. There, at Hancock

Creek, was also one of the best swimming holes ever.

Annie and George Russell met in Virginia and married in 1895. George's parents, Edward D. and Sarah Meadows Russell, already lived at Havelock, and the young couple joined them there in 1897. Their first child, Anthony Joseph, was born the following year.

Edward Russell (1840-1902) was from Jones County. At Havelock, he was a farmer and served as magistrate and postmaster. His wife, Sarah, was born in England. The Edward Russell home was near where the Atlantic Baptist Association is today on Greenfield Heights Boulevard. He died of smallpox and, due to community health concerns, was buried in his own backyard.

In 1899, while Annie and George Russell were on a horse and buggy trip to attend Catholic Mass in New Bern, their home in Havelock was destroyed by fire. A friend of the family, B.D. Borden, offered the Russells a couple of acres near the landing at Cherry Point. The rest of the Russell children, Edward, Madge, Mary Lillian (the future Mrs. Lillian Trader) and Helen, were born at the family's new home there.

Annie, a strong Irish Catholic, had converted George early on and by 1912 their neighbor, Mr. Borden, had joined the church as well. The story is told that the neighbors would travel up the Neuse River by boat to attend services at St. Paul's Catholic Church in downtown New Bern.

According to a church history by Rev. Robert Ippolito, the first Catholic service held locally was the funeral of the Russell's second child, ten year old Edward Borden Russell, who died in 1911. The child's cause of death is unknown to us. His namesake, B.D. Borden, would later join him in the community cemetery at Cherry Point landing.

Borden, age 76, drowned accidentally in the Neuse on January 18, 1923. The son of Frank Borden, he was a widower at the time of his death.

Following an extended illness, Annie Breslin Russell, 63, died June 12, 1935, about three years after her post office at Cherry Point closed. Her husband, Captain George, followed her one year and two days later. They are buried side-by-side in the little family plot with relatives and neighbors.

There was, and in some local quarters still is, a long-held, often-spoken belief that "there was nothing here before the base was built." This phrase was repeated so many times for so many years that it began to be taken as common wisdom. As we have seen, nothing could be further from the truth. In point of fact, the Havelock district has been crawling with people for more than 300 years.

In 1992, the State of North Carolina erected one of its gray and black historical markers at Cherry Point's Gate Six on the intersection of Cunningham and Fontana boulevards. The marker commemorates the establishment of the Cherry Point Marine Corps Air Station in 1941.

During the dedication ceremony, Cherry Point's commanding general, David Richwine, noted the sacrifice of those who gave their homes to make way for the coming of the base. Many newcomers assume that the land where the base is located was an empty quarter of nothing but woods and wildlife. In fact, 42 families, most black, were forced from their farms and woodland homes in 1940 in preparation for the massive federal building project.

Photographs taken under government contract the following summer show the abandoned structures on the 11,000 acres where some of the families had lived for generations. There were people here; families living simple lives. But as the war approached these people of Havelock, living in communities with names like Nelsontown and Little Witness, were unceremoniously evicted.

They left behind homes and barns and fields with crops still in them. They left behind hog lots, chicken yards, orchards, ponds, docks, and many, many memories.

They also left behind the dead.

The headstones are nestled in the woods today, carved mostly of white marble. These headstones resting beneath graceful trees tell tales of the early days of Havelock. Cemeteries with their engraved stones dot the entire vicinity giving testimony to the fact that thousands of people, black and white, have lived and died here since the time Carolina was a colony of England.

On MCAS Cherry Point today are 17 old cemeteries that archaeologists say are our most informative historic sites. Cemetery Number Nine contains the graves of people who were alive at the same time as George Washington and Thomas Jefferson.

Stephen Winn, for example, was born in 1787, and he and his wife, Elizabeth, were here when the British threatened the region during the War of 1812. When he died in 1833 and was buried on the banks of Slocumb's Creek, Andrew Jackson was President of the United States.

Times were tough. Bryan and Sarah Jones buried a daughter in 1843. Little Elizabeth was 17 months old when she died. Five years later, the Joneses mourned the loss of another child, Martha, barely a year old at her death. A third baby, Gilley, not quite two, was buried by the same parents in 1850. Baby Gilley's grave bears this inscription:

Farewell, lovely babe, farewell,
With me thou canst no longer dwell.
I hope ere long with thee to tell,
That Jesus has done all things well.

Older graves exist in other plots. Many are now unmarked. The oldest marked graves belong to Evan and Sally Jones, descendents of our original settlers. Sally was born in 1761 and was buried on a hill overlooking the Neuse River in 1813. Evan, aged 60, died four years later and was laid beside his wife. Born here in 1757, he was 19 years old at the beginning of the American Revolution.

The carvings and inscriptions on local headstones tell us a great deal about our historical ancestors. The orientation of the graves speaks to the religious heritage of these people. In each instance, the marked graves at Cherry Point are oriented with the headstone toward the west and the footstones toward the east. Christian tradition holds that this makes certain the deceased face the eastern sky, the direction from which the glory of resurrection is expected to come.

The government photographs taken in 1941 do not show the graveyards. The images made near the end of the Great Depression do show that some of the homes were rude and simple, not much more than shacks, like one owned by Joshua Hill where the family's beloved trees continued to bloom and bear fruit after they moved away.

Others were more prosperous and elaborate like the big, substantial home of the Walter Nelson family, left empty in the middle of an untended farm field, surrounded by new barns and a number of sturdy outbuildings.

Nearby, Walter's son, Fred, had just proudly moved his young family into their brand new home when the government agent arrived, legal papers in

Old gravestone at Cherry Point

Edward Ellis Collection

hand, telling them they would have to leave for the good of the nation. He would later receive $500 in payment for his house and land.

Few would argue that the Cherry Point Marine Corps Air Station should not have been built. It was vital to the defense effort during World War II, especially for flight training and in suppressing Nazi submarine warfare off the Carolina coast. It has been a blessed economic boon to a multi-county swath and continues to be one of the most important military bases in the nation. But when you see the marker outside Gate Six, you may wish to remember the local folks who gave so much to make it possible.

19
A New Morning

*W*hat would become the sprawling Marine base at Cherry Point had been under construction for only a few months when the Japanese bombed Pearl Harbor on December 7, 1941. The attack sped up what was already a project on a fast track. Within months, the first of some 20,000 Marines were on their way here.

Like Rip Van Winkle, our little crossroads sprang from its traditional slumber and has buzzed with activity ever since. The bright spot for those displaced from their homes was that members of all but two of the families received jobs related to base construction and operation.

Among the long list of changes that took place in the next few years was the virtual end of the illegal bootlegging business. When base commanders learned that the first homes out of town in almost all directions had illegal liquor for sale they began to cooperate with local law enforcement in a manner that might be considered a violation of the Posse Comitatus statute today. This federal legal principle has been interpreted as limiting the involvement of the U.S. military in civilian law enforcement.

The legal lines were fuzzy here for a long time. Into the 1960s, air station resources were used to provide fire and rescue service to the civilian community and military policemen patrolled in the same vehicles with civilian law officers. For nearly 20 years there was an MP station in New Bern to handle wayward sailors and Marines.

So it is not surprising that Marine bosses authorized the use of their helicopters to hover above local woods and spot moonshine stills from the air. The distillation process for moonshine moved relatively quickly, but it does produce smoke. The main vulnerability lies in the long fermentation process when an assortment of watertight boxes sits on the ground for many days making a profile, hard to find on foot, but easily visible from above.

These "training exercises" by Marine helicopter crews coordinated by radio with state law enforcement officers on the ground were highly successful resulting in some arrests, destruction of numerous illegal stills and the creation of a strong disincentive for operators to stay in the business. We can rationalize the questionable legality of the matter, if necessary, by saying that these were simpler times. And besides, the moonshiners were in no position to cry foul.

A number of factors led to the demise of the local bootlegging business. The end of Prohibition brought a steady supply of legal booze courtesy of state-owned stores. The reputation for the high quality of Craven County Corn began to deteriorate. A major factor was that jobs were now readily available courtesy of our kindly Uncle Sam.

In a single month in the summer of 1941, 800 people were hired at once and the numbers increased by the day until 8,000 workers were engaged in the construction project. Many were paid the then-princely sum of 40 cents per hour. By the time the first of 310 planes landed at the new "Cunningham" airfield, named for the first marine aviator, Alfred A. Cunningham, on March 18, 1942, huge amounts of money were flowing into the local economy.

The initial budget of $25 million soon zoomed to $82 million.

The construction of Cherry Point has been called "one of the most colossal building programs" of World War II. One historian said that "the amount of paving completed at Cherry Point was perhaps greater than any other place at one time in the history of mankind." It equaled 269 miles of 20-foot wide highway. Enough timber was cut to create 5,000,000 board feet of lumber. Twenty million bricks were laid. Ten million cubic yards of earth were moved. During the 18 months of initial construction of the base, some 1,800 permanent buildings and 2,500 temporary structures were built. That is an average of 7.9 buildings per day. At one point, the story goes, four buildings were finished per hour. In the process, 50,000,000 board feet of lumber was used.

One observer called it "controlled chaos."

Overseeing the construction whirlwind was Navy Lt. Cmdr. E.W.C. Nice who arrived with a team of three other officers on July 28, 1941. Nice immediately established temporary construction headquarters in the finest hotel available, the Queen Anne on Broad Street in New Bern. Close behind the Navy builders came Cherry Point's first Marine command: Lt. Col. Thomas J. Cushman and four enlisted men. Cushman, from Missouri, joined the Marines in 1917 and became a pilot the following year.

The terrain of Cherry Point's swamps, farms and forest was so rugged that a former traveling candy salesman turned government inspector named Dick Parker initially did his job riding on horseback.

He would ride the local boom as well later becoming one of the area's most successful automobile dealers.

The 36-month construction of this incredible military city in the most barren land George Washington ever beheld required the laying of 23 miles of drainage pipe, 26 miles of water mains, and 25 miles of electrical lines.

People were pouring in by the thousands. Housing was at a premium and infrastructure did not always keep up with demand. A dog-eared medical officer's report from the period shows that one newly built temporary barracks was being used simultaneously as a clinic, a chapel and a beer hall. Primary power for the station bakery was initially provided by a railroad locomotive. And the first quarters for a newly arrived Navy corpsman, my father, Ed Ellis, age 17, was a mattress under a stairwell at the brand-new Naval Dispensary.

But, at long last, in Havelock times got easier.

Work, once scarce to nonexistent in our neck of the woods, became plentiful. Along with the Marines came Overhaul & Repair (O&R), later called the Naval Air Rework Facility (NARF), now the Naval Aviation Depot (NADEP). Besides construction, and a myriad of other civil service slots, O&R employed thousands of local residents in well-paying, steady, recession-proof jobs.

Yep, many a local moonshiner took a job "on the base." With less demand and other economic opportunities, most chose another way to make a living. For many bootleggers, those helicopters were simply the last straw.

The rest, as they say, is history.

Cherry Point, the world's largest Marine Corp air station, became the Number One employer in eastern North Carolina. The Marines brought with them a more modern world view than had existed here previously. Havelock grew culturally apart from some other nearby towns and cities becoming more an international crossroads than a typical Southern town. Marines, world travelers themselves, moved here from every state in the nation, bringing with them attitudes, ideas and customs foreign to a community recently emerged from a 100-year time capsule.

Unexpectedly, a new day dawned here and things were never to be the same. A closed community slowly began to open. The southern accent waned a little. And people from everywhere began to adopt Havelock as home.

Havelock does not look typical either. The people who originally settled here were rural and built homes and other buildings out of the readily available trees. They were spread out on farms and plantations. New Bern, in contrast, was built by city people who laid out a city and built with more permanent materials like brick, especially after the mid-1850s. They concentrated their building because they wanted to be able to walk about easily as walking was the main form of transportation in the 1700s.

Most of "modern" Havelock was built out of anything at hand in a few short years in the 1940s and 1950s. It was a boom town. The population of Township Six, which includes and surrounds Havelock, went from 723 people in 1940 to 11,695 in 1950, and 18,053 in 1960. And the town was built in the time of the automobile, thus, the conventional walking downtown was simply not a necessity.

Housing was not created quickly enough for the influx of new citizens. One solution was the numerous trailer parks that sprouted throughout town and on its outskirts.

In 1940, one report shows, Havelock proper had just 24 homes and about 100 residents. With the help of Cherry Point, it grew to be the most populace city in Craven County and the surrounding counties as well.

After six years of legal wrangling and rancorous, uproarious debate, it incorporated in 1959 with a mayor and council to become the Town of Havelock.

Havelock leaders receive town charter from Secretary of State Thad Eure in Raleigh, August 24, 1959.
From left, seated, Mayor George Griffin, Eure, Commissioner Reuel Lee. Standing, attorney Kennedy Ward, Commissioner Irving Beck, Commissioner Clay Wynne, and business leaders Ray Vawter and Dick Flye.

Edward Ellis Collection

On August 24, 1959, a local delegation went to Raleigh to receive the town charter. The group photographed in Secretary of State Thad Eure's office was made up of the winners of the fight for incorporation. With 336 of 353 qualified voters casting ballots, they had won by 35 votes. Such election "landslides" would become typical of Havelock politics in the years to come.

The assemblage that day included George Griffin, Havelock's first mayor, and Commissioners Reuel S. Lee, Irving Beck and Clay Wynne. Commissioners Jesse Lewis and Norwood Sanders were absent that day. Others there were Town Attorney Kennedy Ward and leaders of the Havelock Retail Merchants Association, Ray Vawter and Dick Flye. Three members of the town board were Cherry Point employees.

The military base was humming. The town was growing. Highway 70's serpentine route through Havelock was straightened, made four lanes and renamed "Main Street." Once again, the township was crawling with people and more were coming every day.

Looking back it is easy to see now why people who came to Havelock in the 1920s thought they were among the first to get here. People who came here in the 1930s thought the same thing. Even folks who arrived at the dawning of the Marine base had no reason to suspect that so much had gone on here over the previous 250 years.

Now you know.

Nevertheless, there are plenty of other untold stories and many local people unaccounted for. I told you in the beginning that history is always incomplete. There are dozens of people from the modern era who deserve a good telling of their stories. There are businessmen, educators, and lawmen, social, civic and government leaders, coaches and volunteers, war heroes and a few rascals, all of whom need to be added formally to our written local history.

Maybe at some moment in the future we can get together again to share more of our collective story. Until then, remember these tales of Havelock and eastern Craven County.

Remember that as a community, we have been here more than 300 years. We have had Indian wars, a struggle for independence, and a civil war. We were invaded and occupied. We have claimed as our own the name of one of the great characters of world history. We were made prosperous and even wealthy as the focal point of the international exporting of naval stores. We have been impoverished by depression, and, by necessity, become for a while a community populated by bootlegging outlaws. And then, as if by magic, this small place has become the home of the Second Marine Air Wing.

Most of all let us remember forever the most important lesson of history. As we have seen here, anything—anything!—can happen.

And it probably will.

20

Tidbits, Morsels & Leftovers

*S*omeone told me a history of Havelock could not be written without mentioning Babe Ruth. So here you go: Babe Ruth.

Only kidding.

Fact is, Babe Ruth, along with New York Giants pitcher Christie Mathewson, and nationally known cartoonist Bud Fisher and other celebrities often enjoyed the hunting, fishing, liquor and ladies in these parts. "The Bambino" was a frequent guest at Camp Bryan, down Nine Mile Road, now called Lake Road, and was often seen around Gray Road where there was a lot of "industrial activity," if you know what I mean.

Everybody in Havelock from that era claims "The Babe" stayed with them.

One of the best cemeteries in Havelock proper, where many of the recent "old-timers" are buried, is behind the circa 1886 First United Methodist Church on Miller Boulevard. I am not suggesting you go snooping around uninvited, but that's where it is.

Yet another curiosity of history: That half-moon shaped point of land at the mouth of Slocum Creek, described in Chapter 14 as an important home of the Neusiok Indians in 1711, is the same vicinity where Union general Burnside unloaded his troops in 1862 during the War Between the States.

Reno, Nevada is named for Union Gen. Jesse L. Reno, one of Burnside's commanders who landed at Slocum Creek. Reno was a Mexican War hero and was killed in a Civil War battle in Maryland a few months after the Battle of New Bern. The Nevada river crossing on the Central Pacific Railroad was named in his honor in 1868.

The man who commanded local Confederate forces in the defense of New Bern was Brig. Gen. Lawrence O'Bryan Branch. By the time of the Battle of New Bern, Branch had graduated from UNC Chapel Hill, owned and edited a newspaper, become an attorney and practiced law, been president of a railroad, served in the U.S. House of Representatives and had been appointed to and declined the office of Secretary of the U.S. Treasury. At the start of the Civil War, he offered his services to his home state of North Carolina. Though outgunned and outmanned in the loss of New Bern, he was considered a "rising star" among Southern generals. Just six months after the battle here Branch died instantly from a gunshot wound to the face while leading troops in battle at Antietam.
He was only 33 years old.

Another historical curiosity: Reno and Branch died in battle in Maryland within three days of each other and only a few miles apart in September 1862.

Bern, or berne, as in New Bern and Berne, Switzerland, means "bear." New Bern bears, get it?

Bootlegging Era Humor: Little Johnny's daddy wanted to show him the dangers of moonshine. He called the boy to a bench out back of the house where he had placed a glass jar of the potent, clear liquid. Holding a wriggling fishing worm between two fingers, Johnny's father said, "Son, I want to learn you something about white whiskey." The man held the worm over the jar's mouth and dropped it in the liquor. The worm wiggled even more violently at first, but by the time it sank to the bottom it was no longer moving and was obviously dead. The boy watched the whole process. Seriously, the father asked, "Well, son, what does that teach you? Little Johnny looked studiously at the jar. "That's sure a good one, Pa," he said. "What you just learnt me is that people who drink white whiskey don't have worms."

In the mid-1700s the Spanish attacked Beaufort. Hundreds of North Carolina militiamen answered the "Spanish Alarm," marched to Beaufort and repulsed the invaders. The musket-toting force traveled down the Beaufort Road passing through Slocumb's Creek, the future Havelock, both coming and going.

Pure opinion: If a statue or monument is ever built in this city for anyone other than Maj. Gen. Sir Henry Havelock, it should be for Congressman Graham A. Barden. Without Graham Barden, there would be 200 of us here today and we would be commuting across the river each day to work at the Minnesott Marine Corps air base.

A good local put-down: You may be Southern, but you ain't any Comfort.

Now, from colonial records, here's your Separation of Church and State segment:

State of North Carolina, Craven County, April Term, 1815. The jurors on their oath, present that Edmund Blank, not having the fear of God before his eyes, but roused by the hope of gain, did on the 26th day of March, being the Christian Sabbath, commonly called Sunday, cause to be run, within sight of the Town of New Bern on the main road, with certain men to us their names unknown, a Horse Race, to the great danger of peaceable travelers and against the peace and dignity of the State. Signed: H. Carraway, foreman, Meshack Always, John Jones, Claiborn Ivey, Joseph Bell, et al.

Remember: The Havelock district, known by the very earliest settlers as "Neuse" and "Neuse River," later as Slocumb's Creek, was settled before New Bern was founded in 1710.

Havelock got its name in 1857. It incorporated as a town 102 years later in 1959. It became the City of Havelock in 1972.

The man with the coolest job in colonial Craven County was the printer, James Davis of New Bern. He got to print the money. Funny thing, but he became very rich. Owned land all over. One of the places was on Slocum Creek where he had a water-powered sawmill. In 1764, Davis advertised in his newspaper, *The North Carolina Gazette*, for someone to tend the mill for him. He also sought a millwright to build another mill on the same creek with a "tumbling dam," where the water flows over the top. Could this be the origin of Spaight's Mill from Chapter 10?

Beaufort was founded in 1722 and was originally called Fishtown. Wilmington, first known as New Liverpool, was established in 1730. It had the deepest entry from the ocean, about 18 feet, and soon became the state's commercial center.

Locally retired Coast Guard Rear Admiral Edwin H. Daniels informed us that the first Coast Guard air station was opened at Morehead City in 1920. Using Curtis HS-2L Flying Boats, the fliers located derelict ships and those in distress until funding ran out and the station closed in July, 1921.

For those who are interested in numbers, Slocum Creek, the location of Havelock Station, is at railroad milepost 75.7. The distance is measured from the line's starting point at Goldsboro.

Our Slocumb family descended from "Old Anthony" Slocumb of Albemarle County, N.C. He was a Lords Proprietor deputy who died at an advanced age, possibly 99, in 1690. Tracking the Slocumbs will drive you crazy. There was a father, son and grandson all named John. The three John Slocumbs were alive here simultaneously doing things with land and the courts. Then there was Josiah, Joshua and Josias, and the whole bunch of them liked to sign their names Jo. Slocumb. Just lovely!

Early last century, Riverdale's Thurman School was located near the current site of the National Forest Ranger Station on U.S. 70. At the same time, the Croatan School stood where the Croatan Presbyterian Church is now.

The first Catholic Mass at Havelock was held in a rail car. In 1928, Father Egbert Albert arrived here in the "St. Peter's Chapel Car." The mobile missionary in his rolling church spent several days on a railroad siding near the Havelock depot ministering to the faithful.

In the 746-page volume "A History of New Bern and Craven County" by Alan Watson and published in 1987 by the Tryon Palace Commission, Havelock is mentioned 12 times. Kinston, in Lenoir County, is mentioned 26 times. Beaufort, in Carteret County, is mentioned 60 times. Otherwise, it's a dandy book.

Before the founding of this country, John Tucker settled and claimed land along a branch of Slocumb's Creek that bears his name today: Tucker Creek.

Anderson Creek, another branch of Slocumb's Creek, marked the edge of the 2,000-acre Magnolia Plantation, owned by John Lovick. Lovick, a colonial surveyor, received a grant for the land in 1719. He and his brother, Thomas, were part of a colony of Welsh Quakers who settled along Slocum, Hancock and Clubfoot creeks in 1710. Lovick was a member of the North Carolina Boundary Commission in 1728 that established the permanent border between Virginia and North Carolina. He built his plantation home on or near what is now the 15th fairway of the Carolina Pines golf course. Local tradition holds that the Lovick family's grand mansion there was burned by Union forces during the Civil War.

In 1713, a man named John Harlow bought land on a creek of the Newport River. Yep, that's Harlowe.

Maximum irony: The French Huguenots fled France where some of them had been the victims of religious and political massacres. They crossed an ocean and built homes in the New World of Craven County where some of them became the victims of Indian massacres.

The book about Francisco de Miranda, *The New Democracy in America,* translated by Judson P. Wood, and published by the University of Oklahoma Press, is still in print and can easily be ordered on the Internet.

Observation: In the beginning Havelock depended on a single-engine economy, naval stores, and went bust. Next this community depended on a single-engine economy, bootlegging, and was busted. Today Havelock relies on a single-engine economy, a military base. What's that thing they say about people who don't learn the lessons of history being doomed to repeat it?

Don't forget: A Time Capsule is underground just outside the Havelock Public Safety Building. Buried in 1984 at the 25th anniversary of Havelock's incorporation, it is to be opened July 25, 2034.

THE HAVELOCK HISTORICAL COLLECTION

Historical records in the possession of the author will one day be donated to the permanent collection of one of the libraries of the University of North Carolina system. Hundreds of documents and photographs collected by the author over several decades, including the material on which this book is based, will be preserved.

The final selection of the location of the Havelock Historical Collection will hinge on two factors: the resources the chosen university offers in the care and cataloguing of the material and the ease of its availability to both researchers and the interested public.

A limited amount of the material related to Cherry Point is now in the permanent collection of the Joyner Library at East Carolina University, Greenville, N.C. It is listed there as the Edward Barnes Ellis, Jr. Papers.

Mr. Ellis believes his entire collection belongs to the citizens of the Havelock area and must be preserved for future generations.

Many of the documents, artifacts and photographs now in the hands of the author have been contributed by local individuals and families. All donated material is labeled by source. Contributions related to the Havelock area and eastern Craven County are welcome.

All material will be considered. Of particular interest are pre-Cherry Point family histories and genealogies, portraits, journals, diaries, deeds, brochures, publications, maps and business records. Also sought are early photos, especially of people, events, economic activity and local buildings, such as churches, schools and stores. Provisions for the copying of photographs and documents can be made at no expense to the donor.

Any reader wishing to consider a contribution of historical material to be permanently preserved in the collection is urged to write to Havelock Historical Collection, 7001 Jeffrey Drive, Raleigh, N.C. 27603 or log on to www.havelockhistory.com.

About the Author

Edward Barnes Ellis, Jr. has worked as a journalist, a lobbyist and a laborer. A native of Craven County, Eddie is the descendant of a family that recorded the first land deed in North Carolina. Among his ancestors are settlers at Jamestown, Va., and veterans of the American Revolution and the War Between the States.

He served in the N.C. General Assembly for four years as a legislative representative for state employees. For many years, he was engaged in the newspaper business as a reporter, photographer, columnist, editor and publisher. Eddie is the founder of the *Havelock News* and the former publisher of Cherry Point's *Windsock*. He was chosen to be the official historian of the City of Havelock in 1984.

Eddie and his wife, Veronica, are now residential and commercial real estate developers.

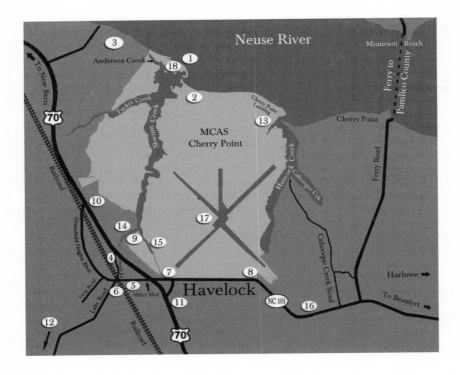

Key to Map:

1. Burnside Landing 1862
2. Cherry Point Officers' Club
3. Magnolia Plantation/Carolina Pines
4. Civil War Blockhouse Fort
5. Railroad Depot & Traders Store
6. Old Depot Site
7. Main Gate/MCAS
8. "Little Witness" or Melvin, N.C.
9. Graham A. Barden Elementary School
10. Westbrook Shopping Center
11. Havelock City Hall
12. Camp Bryan
13. Hancock Boat Docks
14. West prong of Slocum Creek
15. East prong of Slocum Creek
16. Approximate location of Always Inn
17. MCAS Runways
18. Neusiok Indian Village

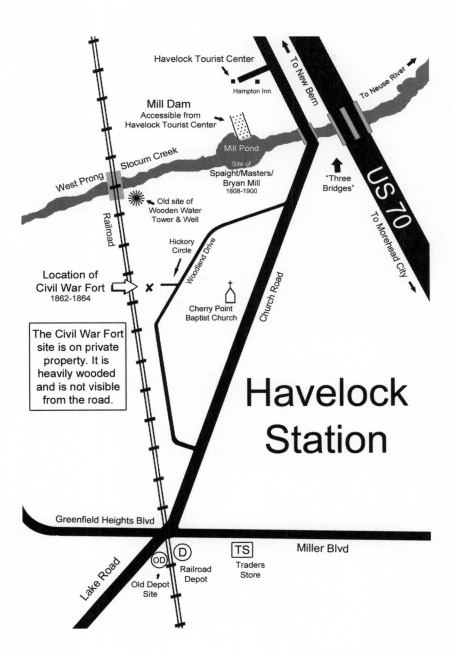

To order additional copies of
In This Small Place

McBryde Publishing
108 Dogwood Lane
New Bern, North Carolina USA
1-877-830-0759
www.mcbrydepublishing.com

Or go to:

www.edwardellis.com

For additional local historical
information, go to:

www.havelockhistory.com